By Oscar Handlin

◨◨◨◨

Fire-Bell in the Night

THE CRISIS IN CIVIL RIGHTS

Fire-Bell in the Night

THE CRISIS IN CIVIL RIGHTS

□□□□□□□□□□□□□□□□□

by Oscar Handlin

An Atlantic Monthly Press Book

LITTLE, BROWN AND COMPANY · BOSTON · TORONTO

Parts of this book originally appeared in somewhat different form in the *Atlantic Monthly*, to whom credit is due.

ATLANTIC-LITTLE, BROWN BOOKS
ARE PUBLISHED BY
LITTLE, BROWN AND COMPANY
IN ASSOCIATION WITH
THE ATLANTIC MONTHLY PRESS

*Published simultaneously in Canada
by Little, Brown & Company (Canada) Limited*

PRINTED IN THE UNITED STATES OF AMERICA

For Edward Weeks
affectionately

This momentous question, like a fire-bell in the night, awakened and filled me with terror. I considered it at once as the knell of the Union. It is hushed, indeed, for the moment. But this is a reprieve only . . . We have the wolf by the ears, and we can neither hold him, nor safely let him go.

— THOMAS JEFFERSON, writing in 1820, when the question of the statehood of Missouri had turned men's attention to the anomalous status of slavery in the Republic.

Contents

Fire-Bell in the Night

THE CRISIS IN CIVIL RIGHTS

1

□ □ □ □

An Unfinished Task

FOR a few weeks in a stunned nation the hope flickered
that President Kennedy's assassination might, after all,
be the occasion for a breakthrough in the interracial strife.
Perhaps enactment of a program that meant much to him
would give meaning to his martyrdom. Public opinion polls
in December showed that Americans felt a sense of personal remorse and a guilty consciousness that they had
done too little to further the spirit and practice of brotherhood. More specifically, an impressive percentage of them
connected the tragedy in Dallas with the need for advanc-
ing the status of the Negro.

But when the emotion of the aftermath drained away,
it became clear that no miracle had occurred. President
Johnson did indeed persuade Representative Howard Smith
of Virginia, chairman of the House Rules Committee, to
begin hearings on the civil rights bill in January. Yet as
those at last lumbered toward a conclusion, it was apparent
that the alignments of a year before had hardly changed.

Meanwhile, the tenth anniversary of the Supreme Court's
ruling against school segregation approached. In May 1954
a unanimous decision had struck down the concept of "separate but equal" that for sixty years had sustained the inferior position of the Negro. At the time, the Court's ruling
seemed the start of a genuine social revolution, coming as
it did after a long series of lesser gains. There were grounds

then for the belief that ancient wrongs would steadily be righted. A decade later, the outcome is still not certain. The place of the Negro in American life has changed significantly, but the consequences have not been those anticipated in 1954.

All too many Americans were lulled into inactivity by the belief that progress toward equality was inevitable and, given time enough, would take its own course. They should have known better. Equality was never a gift bestowed upon the passive; it could be won by struggle and lost by inertia. The Negro gained in civic and social rights in the decade after the end of the Civil War; he voted, held office and had access to educational institutions. But in the 1880's, when he ceased to advance, he fell backward. That experience should have been a warning in 1954. It should sound an alarm in 1964.

This volume is an effort at stocktaking. It does not purport to set down the complete historical record of the past decade, or even to supply a full narrative of the dramatic events of those years. It contains, simply, the reflections of an observer who hopes that a reasoned analysis will help his countrymen solve one of the great problems of their time.

At the heart of the problem was the breathtaking aspiration of the founders of the Republic to create a free nation out of a population of diverse origins that was already heterogeneous and that would soon spread across an immense continent. It quickly became apparent that, among such people, liberty would be secure only if associated with equality. Men would respect those rights of others which they themselves shared. The inequalities of some could only be preserved by hedging about the freedom of others.

Americans have never completely realized the ideals of the Founders. But those ideals nevertheless remain the only basis on which the Republic is viable. From the start, the peculiar status of the Negro created the most conspicuous discrepancy. Cultural differences, the visibility of a markedly distinctive skin color and a long history of enslavement withheld from the black men the rights to freedom and equality accorded to other Americans. The extended struggle over this issue helped plunge the nation into a fratricidal war and continued unabated in the century thereafter. It approached a new point of crisis ten years ago when the Supreme Court gave its decision in the case of *Brown* v. *Board of Education*.

That ruling settled one crucial issue. It forbade the states to use segregation, as some of them had, to confine the Negro to a position of inferiority. It and subsequent judgments demanded the destruction "with all deliberate speed" of the complex pattern of separate institutions which deprived black Americans of equality of opportunity and diminished their freedom. In considerable measure, the progress of the Negroes since 1954 has reflected the impact of that decision.

The advances toward equality in this decade, however gratifying, nevertheless may not have been speedy enough. The rate of economic and social change in the United States is so rapid that a handicapped group falls ever further behind if it progresses more slowly than the rest of the population. Delays now are more costly than in more leisurely eras; and there may not be much time left to act without excessive social damage.

By what means and toward what ends should action come? The tactics of the struggle in the past ten years have confused the answers. Because segregation enforced by law was long an instrument to oppress the Negro, integration became the primary objective of Americans concerned with equality. Any kind of separateness whether legal or voluntary was suspect as a mask for prejudice and discrimination. Integration alone could assure equality in the North as well as in the South. The ultimate goal was a society that wiped out all racial, indeed all group, distinctions.

On this point, there is a curious convergence of opinions at the extremes. Those who oppose equality because it leads to amalgamation and those who favor amalgamation as a guarantee to equality join in the belief that there is no alternative: men are either all the same or they are unequal. People who go to school, or reside, or work side by side must inevitably fuse. All other questions, from this perspective, become subsidiary to those of intermarriage and miscegenation. To the white supremacist as to the total assimilationist, the choice therefore is between freezing the status quo or an immediate total revolution, genetic as well as social.

Such statements of the issue are false! We can be equal and different — in color as in creed or national origin. Whatever the remote future may hold for the population of the United States, the foreseeable future will still find its people marked off from one another by the character of their antecedents. The color of the Negro will not soon bleach away, as certain romantic well-wishers once thought it would; and even were some magic of biochemistry to make that possible, psychological, social and cultural differences would still persist for generations. And there is no reason why they should not! A dark skin is not a disease, as Benjamin Rush thought it was. Nor need the colored man or woman wish to obliterate the memory of his heritage; surely in our scale of values it is not more disgraceful to have sprung from ancestors who were slaves than to have descended from those who were brutal slaveholders. All skin colors are associated with both degrading and ennobling antecedents: George Washington was white but so was Benedict Arnold. Shade of pigmentation alone gives no American sufficient grounds for either pride or shame.

Integration and equality are not identical. It has not been necessary in the past to wipe out all group distinctions in order to afford each individual equality of opportunity in the pursuit of the advantages of American life. Nor need it be in the future.

In the task that lies ahead it is less important to ascribe the blame for past errors than to locate the responsibility for future decisions. Americans have been endowed with a complex heritage which they can use or misuse. It includes preconceptions, habits and special privileges which have earlier trapped them into tragic mistakes. It includes also liberating ideas that can guide them in the continuing process of creating the free society of which the Founders dreamed.

One thing is certain: now, no more than a century ago, will this nation be able to endure half free. The new release of freedom will have to be extended to all the people. The stakes are equally crucial for every American. No one, no matter how fortunate, can feel secure in rights that are denied to some; and no one, no matter how oppressed, can expect any larger hope for freedom than that which can result from fulfillment of the promises of the Republic — a society governed by consent with liberty and justice for all.

II

Toward Equality — At What Speed?

B Y most conventional measurements, the Negro has made tremendous progress in the decade since 1954. Leaving aside for the moment the more complex question of whether his gains have been fast enough or wide enough, a survey of his advances is certainly impressive; and the variety of the fields in which they have occurred supplies a reasonable basis for the expectation that they will continue.

The colored people of the United States have gained a power they never before enjoyed, and they have steadily raised the level of their education, employment and standards of living. If their grievances nevertheless remain and are even more intensely felt than before, it is not because these ten years have been empty of achievement but because the approach toward equality has made them eager to go the full distance.

It may seem ironic to list as a gain the acquisition of a minimal sense of personal security. Yet there were single years, within this century, when well over a hundred Negroes were lynched. Although two decades of agitation after 1922 failed to enact a federal antilynching law, the number of these communally organized murders declined steadily, especially after 1930. In the last decade, this technique of terror has not been available to those who wished to keep the blacks in their place. Nor have race riots erupted when relationships became tense as they once did in East St. Louis, Atlanta or Detroit.

The absence of these outbreaks is particularly significant because the Negro is no longer meek and undemanding, but assertive and more provocative than ever before. Nevertheless, despite his challenge to the old order, the rope and faggot have gone out of use. Sensitivity to national opinion, the reluctance to invite federal intervention, better police methods and years of education have all contributed to the growing restraint. And, in addition, even the rowdiest elements in the most backward counties have begun to learn that the potential colored victims are no longer altogether powerless or without the ability to retaliate.

The power of the Negroes is the product of both political and moral influence. For the first time they have become a consequential factor in the decisions of government; and they have developed effective means of appealing to the conscience of the country.

The suffrage came within reach of the colored men when they began to move out of the rural South, where the one-party system and a tight apparatus of control kept them from the ballot box. In 1900, almost 90 per cent of American Negroes lived in the states of the former Confederacy; by 1960 just over 50 per cent were still there. The migration to New York or Chicago or Philadelphia did not work an immediate miracle; the newcomers were often apathetic and they were unacquainted with either the means or objectives of political action. Usually they were first enlisted by the ward machines and they were slow to understand how their votes could be used in their own interests. In that respect they were not unlike earlier migrants to the metropolis. In the 1920's and 1930's, nevertheless, the growing weight of Negro numbers was reflected in the election to office of some colored politicians in the cities of their highest concentration.

Since 1940, the steady increase in the size of their vote

[9]

as the migration out of the South continued has made their support crucial in the key states of the North and the West. No office seeker in New York, Pennsylvania, Illinois, Michigan or California can disregard this sector of the electorate. A place for the Negro has become a normal part of the balanced-ticket tactics of urban politics; and every official in these areas must be sensitive to the wishes of his colored constituents.

Fully as significant for the future are the cracks already perceptible in the solid South. In such states as Georgia and Florida, the election of Negroes to local positions is a dramatic indication of what will come as the franchise spreads to ever larger numbers. There have also been starts, although against heartbreaking obstacles, of voter registration drives deep in the intransigent counties of Alabama and Mississippi. There is a long way to go still before the guarantees of the Fifteenth Amendment that no one be deprived of the suffrage by reason of his race are made effective; but a beginning has at last been made and the new civil rights act may open access to the ballot further and increase still more the weight of the Negro vote.

Any additional weakening of the Southern control system will also help. The steady rise in the 1950's of Republican strength below the Mason-Dixon line is a potential advantage, for it may foreshadow the appearance of a genuine two-party system there. If that development should continue, it would give the colored people added leverage in the quest for political equality. By the same token, the Supreme Court's decision in *Baker* v. *Carr* (1962) is likely to have sweeping consequences. That case, which held that the failure to redistrict was a denial of rights secured by the Fourteenth Amendment, struck down the anachronisms which now favor the country voter and seems certain to increase the representation of the cities and their suburbs. Since the Negroes more often enjoy the suffrage in urban than in rural localities, they will probably have a growing influence upon the state legislatures of the future.

Accordingly, it is not unduly optimistic to look forward to the early end of the Negro's disfranchisement. As he acquires the complete rights of a citizen, he will increasingly have the means for insisting that he be treated as an equal.

Changes in Negro organizations within the past decade have revealed how his newly acquired power can be used. A variety of competently led groups, using a wide range of tactical weapons, now mobilize his efforts.

In 1954 the National Association for the Advancement of Colored People and the Urban League shouldered the whole burden. These agencies had been at work for almost a half-century. Their services were necessary and had produced some measure of amelioration. But they were approaching the point at which a revaluation of their objectives was essential.

The two bodies had operated largely through the conventional tactics of litigation and negotiation. The Urban League, concerned with social welfare as well as with civil rights, had focused on the problems of employment. Its tone was moderate, its method undramatic and its results unspectacular. The NAACP had been considered the more radical of the two. Its energies were dedicated to the quest for legislative and judicial relief. It had labored in vain for a federal antilynching law; and it had lobbied, with more success, for state and local laws to prevent discrimination. But its most important activity had been in the courts. The cases it fought had been in good part responsible for the gains the Negro had persistently made in fifty years of agitation. The school desegregation decision of 1954 seemed the climax of its efforts.

Disappointment in the aftermath inevitably called for a reconsideration both within the organizations and among Negroes generally. The problems of enforcement, which became clear in the next three years, raised serious questions about the adequacy of the old tactics. It would take generations to fight district by district through the courts;

and it was hard to counsel patience to those who had already waited too long for equality.

The NAACP and the Urban League had been largely supported by whites and had attracted the attention of only a small minority of the Negroes. After 1954 their methods seemed intolerably slow to the postwar generation of young Negroes not content to sit idly by until the remote future waiting for rights which they felt were due them at once. These more aggressive people formed or joined new groups which not only took on a share of the work but also, indirectly, stimulated the old agencies to renewed activity.

The Congress of Racial Equality (CORE) had been founded in 1942 to apply pacifist methods to the civil rights movement. Its leaders were strongly influenced by Ghandi's theories of nonviolent action, which they merged with the tactics of picketing and the sit-down that unions had used successfully in the 1930's. In the hard days of the depression, when the great corporations had refused to recognize the obligation to bargain collectively imposed by the Wagner Act, the auto workers sat down in the plants and thereby won public support. CORE resolved to do the same. In 1954 it was still a tiny group; not until two years later was it able to hire its first field secretary. Then it began its work in the South, concentrating largely on public accommodations. Its dramatic demonstrations won it quick popularity, which enabled it to expand the scope of its activities to voter registration.

Meanwhile, the bus boycott launched in 1955 by the Montgomery Improvement Association had attracted nationwide attention to the spontaneous protests against Jim Crow practices in various cities of the Deep South. The similarities among these incidents were the result not of a coordinated plan, but of the exclusion of Southern Negroes from any role in making community decisions. In Montgomery as in Birmingham or Tuskegee or Tallahassee, there were no political or social channels through which colored people could work; for those who would not acquiesce in the status quo, the only alternative to brute violence was the boycott and the sit-in. That the choice was passive resistance rather than force was due in large measure to the influence of such young religious leaders as Martin Luther King, Fred L. Shuttlesworth and C. K. Steele, who were the guiding elements in the campaign. In 1957, King was instrumental in drawing together a number of these ministers and their followers in the Southern Christian Leadership Conference.

These developments were tremendously attractive to youth everywhere. In the 1950's there seemed little in the United States that offered young people scope for action that was practical yet idealistic in aim. On many a college campus there was an eager groping for meaningful ways of doing something useful. Many boys and girls of this generation — black and white — felt reluctant to settle down to grubbing for their own careers without making a serious effort to grapple with the world's problems. Here was something specific they could do. They responded with enthusiasm, just as they would respond a little later to the challenge of the Peace Corps.

Student action began spontaneously with a sit-in in Greensboro, North Carolina, in 1960; the movement quickly involved tens of thousands of participants, and within a year it took organizational form in the Student Nonviolent Coordinating Committee (SNCC). Its work has continued with unabated zeal since then.

The mounting strength of the new groups has not weakened but revitalized the old agencies. The running competition for credit and support among the rival participants in the civil rights struggle has some undesirable features, but it also keeps all of them alive to the urgency of action. The Urban League has grown increasingly militant and the NAACP has thrown its weight behind the sit-ins. The younger people in both groups show an increasing tendency toward radicalism on the issue of equality.

Differences in emphasis continue to separate the agencies, but all recognize the primary objective of an immediate advance to equality. Negroes are now the dominant element in these organizations, which are well financed and staffed by a competent bureaucracy. The new techniques of the sit-in and of nonviolent protests have been added to those of political agitation and litigation. As a result, the Negroes' interests are better represented than ever before.

Pressure from these sources has already produced striking improvement. The Negroes' problems are far from solved, but a measurable distance has been covered in the approach toward equality in education, employment, housing and in access to public accommodations.

There has been a marked rise in the quality of education available to colored children. Seven states which had maintained segregated systems before 1954 have made noticeable progress. In Delaware, West Virginia, Maryland, the District of Columbia, Kentucky, Missouri and Oklahoma, 80 to 100 per cent of the school districts are integrated and substantial numbers of black boys and girls now sit in the same classrooms with whites. In Florida, North Carolina, Tennessee, Virginia and Texas, integration has been accepted as public policy; between 10 and 25 per cent of the districts have actually taken the step, although the number of students involved is still small. In Arkansas, Georgia and Louisiana there has been.token compliance with the law; fewer than 5 per cent of the districts have moved in this direction. Only Alabama, Mississippi and South Carolina remain totally intransigent.

The Northern states have begun to deal with their own version of the problem, which arises not from segregation by law but from the residential distribution that in effect creates separate Negro schools. New York City's open enrollment plan, for instance, permits parents to shift children from one school to another in the interest of racial balance. Many communities have recognized the need for redrawing district lines to take in a varied population. The Princeton plan unites the schools of adjoining neighborhoods and allocates children to one building or another by grade rather than by race. Even more important has been a conscientious exploration of the means of compensating for the educational disadvantages of the Negro. The Higher Horizons program sponsored by the New York City Board of Education, for example, has made an active and successful effort to supply in the school the cultural advantages lacking in the homes of the poor; sensitive counseling, intensive reading instruction and visits to museums, the opera and colleges aim to stimulate the students to strive for careers that will help them out of the slums.

The result is apparent in the statistics of school attendance. Practically all Negro children between the ages of seven and thirteen in the United States are now enrolled; twenty years ago, one in five was not.

The ability to take advantage of opportunities for higher education has also increased. All the public and most of the private colleges and universities in every state are now desegregated even if in some cases the action has only token value for the moment; and, in many places, fair educational practice laws forbid racial discrimination among applicants. As a result, about 250,000 colored students study in these institutions — double the number of 1930. For the graduates, the road to professional training is far more open than ever before; indeed, in some cases, there are more places available than qualified applicants to fill them.

Some of the effects have already become visible in employment and have compensated for the dilatoriness of government action. Congress consistently refused to pass a federal fair employment practices act, although executive ordinances have forbidden discrimination in work on government contracts and the President's Committee on Equal Employment Opportunities has persuaded more than a hundred large companies to open up positions to Negroes. The laws of some states also protect the colored job seeker against bias. These measures have been influential insofar as they set up norms approved by the community, but they have been difficult to enforce. In Philadelphia, Chicago and New York, therefore, selective boycotts have put pressure on recalcitrant employers to bring them into line.

But all such regulations depend for success upon the existence of an adequate pool of trained personnel for the desirable places; and the rising level of education has steadily added to that pool. The improvement in skills and the abatement of prejudice have opened opportunities to Negroes that were closed just a decade ago. Colored men and women stand behind the counters of the metropolitan department stores and work in the offices of the banks and insurance companies that once shut their doors to them. The breakthrough has come among supervisory personnel and white-collar employees as well. Eight Southern states and the District of Columbia have desegregated the staffs of their schools; and, throughout the country, the number of colored teachers has risen. More generally a substantial growth in the size of the Negro professional class — engineers and technicians, physicians and lawyers — reflects better schooling. The federal, state and local civil service has been particularly responsive; the number of colored men and women who found such places leaped from about two hundred thousand in 1940 to well over eight hundred thousand in 1960 — about 10 per cent of the total.

The great mass of Negroes remain laborers. Unenviable as their lot is, it too has improved in some respects. About one and a half million of these people left the South to live in the North in the 1950's; and the flow continues. These migrants have thus escaped from the most depressed rural sectors of the economy where their earning capacity was minimal and where there was no hope at all. They face other serious problems in the great cities, but they are no longer bound to the grim futureless condition of unwanted hands in an agriculture that is increasingly mechanized. The persistence of this movement to the urban centers will continue.

The result of the new employment opportunities has

been a noticeable rise in the level of Negro incomes. Although the statistics that bear on this subject command no great confidence, they clearly indicate that the average earnings of colored people have moved steadily upward since the end of the Second World War.

Slowly but demonstrably, the conditions of Negro life have improved. If the life expectancy of "nonwhites" has gone up eight years since the end of the war, that is the result not only of better medical care but also of better diets, more adequate shelter and less hazardous terms of employment. This simple measure of the standard of living is an index of some of the gains of the period.

Urban housing has created troublesome problems for the Negro. His numbers in the United States increased by about 25 per cent in the decade of the 1950's and the course of migration placed the heaviest burden on cities which already suffered from shortages of space. At the same time, paradoxically, urban renewal projects often leveled large tracts of low-rental dwellings and further reduced the amount of available places. In any case, prejudice and relatively low incomes put the colored man at a disadvantage in the competition for quarters and generally compelled him to overpay for what he got.

A concerted effort to destroy discrimination in housing has won victories which for the time being have mostly a symbolic value but may be more significant for the future. The Supreme Court has ruled that restrictive covenants directed at racial and religious minorities may not be enforced in the courts; and fifteen states and many cities forbid bias in housing aided by government funds. Colorado, Connecticut, Massachusetts, New York and Ohio have also made discrimination illegal in most types of private housing. The persistent real estate operator, the biased seller and the hostile neighbor can still devise means of evading the law, but the pressures toward a fairer treatment of the Negro gain in strength.

Meanwhile, the quality of accommodations even in segregated districts receives increasing attention; and in some places, integrated residences offer an escape from the slum. Like the whites, Negroes have spread to the suburbs and have begun to restructure their lives according to middle-class standards.

The struggle for equal access to public facilities has both an immediate and an indirect significance. To be barred by color from lunch counters, restaurants, motels, swimming pools and hotels, to be forced to move to the back of the bus, to be prevented from drinking from a "white" water fountain is an inconvenience and often a hardship. But in addition, all these Jim Crow devices bore, and *were intended to bear*, the imputation of inferiority. They were part of a cumbersome system designed to remind the society that the Negro was a different and a lower type of man. Everywhere, except in the deepest South, these relics of past hatreds are crumbling away before the determined assault, by law or by direct action, of men who know and can show that they are anyone's equal. Significantly, in January 1964 fourteen major Atlanta hotels pledged themselves to accept guests without regard to race — a step that seemed inconceivable only a few years ago.

A new image of the Negro is therefore taking form. Gone is the bumbling stupid caricature of the old tradition. Ever more frequently colored models appear in quality advertising and black faces now form a part of any pictorial representation of the nation. The most eloquent testimony was the comment of the *News-Leader*, a foe of integration, on a sit-in in a Richmond, Virginia, store: "Here were the colored students, in coats, white shirts, ties, and one of them was reading Goethe and one was taking notes from a biology text. And here, on the sidewalk outside, were white youths grinning fit to kill, and some of them, God save the mark, were waving the proud and honored flag of the Southern States in the last war fought by gentlemen." When a howling mob stormed Meredith's dormitory at the University of Mississippi or when the Birmingham police turned the hoses on the marching children, there was no doubt about which were the men worthy of respect. In 1964, a national opinion survey revealed that a distinct majority of Americans no longer thought it inconceivable that they would vote for a Negro for President.

The genuine progress of the past ten years has nevertheless not diminished the sense of grievance among American Negroes. Far from it. The decade since 1954 has witnessed a steady rise in the volume and intensity of their complaints.

The protest continues in part as a result of resentment against the pockets of the country that have made no concessions whatever. Other Americans can push the events in Alabama and Mississippi to the back of their minds; no Negro anywhere can forget that the color of his skin there still exposes him not only to discrimination but to open violence. Murders such as those of Emmett Till and Medgar Evers, more than forty bombings such as those of the Birmingham children, and the harassment of those who wish to register to vote — all unpunished — send recurrent shocks among the more fortunate Negroes who can never enjoy the fruits of their own progress without an awareness of the continued suffering elsewhere of men like themselves.

Lynchings and race riots no longer disgrace American society; and, in the North, Negroes sit not only on juries but on the benches of many courts. Very well! But those gains are no cause for complacency when violence still threatens the colored people of the South who demand equality. And in parts of that region Negroes still do not receive equal treatment at the hands of the law. Despite numerous rulings by the Supreme Court they are excluded from juries, they are subject to prejudicial comment in the argument of cases, and they are not dealt the same justice as whites. The consciousness of these wrongs cuts some of the value out of the progress elsewhere. The exclusion from the ballot that permits clownish mountebanks or sinister demagogues to gain election by agitating the issue of integration injures all the people of Alabama, Mississippi and Louisiana — only the Negroes are more aware of the damage than the whites.

Indeed, the sense of grievance mounts whenever the Negro shifts his sights from the advances that have been made to those which should be made. The statistics which inform him that 10 to 25 per cent of the school districts in the border states have integrated remind him that 75 to 90 per cent, in the ten years since the Supreme Court's decision, have not. And he has legitimate cause for wondering how much of the compliance that has occurred has been only a token in states in which the vast majority of colored and white children still attend separate schools.

Similar questions arise in any estimate of past gains. It is not very gratifying to learn that colored people are better off in the United States than anywhere else in the world when the proper standard of comparison should be with other Americans and not with Asians and Africans. The number of Negro college students has increased but not as much as the number of whites, and there remains a distressing disparity in dropout rates. Average incomes have risen but not as fast as those of whites, and unemployment rates are twice as high. It can be no cause for contentment that one of five Negroes between the ages of sixteen and twenty-one cannot find a job. The life expectancy and standards of living of colored people have gone up, but are still below those of the rest of the population. The genuine gains the Negroes have made in the past decade have only put them in a better position to perceive the gap that still divides them from the other citizens of the Republic.

That gap is real and so provocative that it accounts for much of the sensitivity of Negroes to discussions of their progress. But their resentment also has a psychological basis which explains why what remains to be done looms larger in the thinking of colored Americans than what has actually been achieved.

To begin with, a little progress is a dangerous thing. Speaking of an earlier social upheaval, Tocqueville warned long ago that revolutions are most likely in periods and places where some improvement plants the hope for more among the oppressed. A rising level of expectations increases discontent and makes intolerable the grievances which the utterly hopeless accept as a matter of course. In general, the proximity to equality only excites the hunger for it. The black man is less willing to wait than before because his goal has never been so clearly visible.

The victims of discrimination now are not the children and grandchildren of miserable slaves for whom freedom was a newfound hope. Nor are they immigrants, strangers in a land to whose customs they had to conform. They are Americans who have held a promise of freedom for a century or more and who now feel it is time to collect. Many are veterans who wore the uniform of their country with dignity and who wish, in civilian life, to be treated as the equals they were in the ranks. They have learned, in some places, to be called Mister, to be welcomed in first-class hotels and to find whatever seat they like in the airplane. They see no reason elsewhere to accommodate themselves to the prejudices of the minority that would condemn them to inferiority; and they insist on sharing at once in the opportunities of American life. A ten-year delay seems intolerable.

The militancy of the middle class shows the direction in which the wind is blowing. A generation ago, the black bourgeoisie was docile, content with its own limited gains and willing to accept a world the whites made for it. Often it actually profited from segregation, which provided it with protected opportunities in the closed circle of Negro society. Now the ministers and dentists, the physicians and teachers are in the forefront of the struggle for full equality. Their horizons have widened and they are impatient to get to a still distant shore.

[21]

Others once discriminated against have done it; Negroes can too if the impediments are removed from their way. This is the most significant, although the least recognized, element that enters into the Negro's resentment. He fears that the gap may widen rather than narrow, that he may be permanently left behind, that it is therefore now or never. A subtle change in the past decade has separated the Negro from other Americans and has created a fundamental divergence in experience which unconsciously and unrecognizedly adds a new bitterness to group relations. That change explains why the gains of the past decade are not enough.

III

The Minority Coalition

THE mood of the Negro in 1964 can only be understood in the light of the redefinition of the race problem in the past half-century. His greatest danger today is isolation. In a society which shows increasing tendencies toward accepting as fixed the simple categories of black and white, he may find his experience, interest and attitudes diverging from those of everyone else. One tenth of the nation would then stand arrayed against the other nine tenths in a situation perilous to all.

It was not always thus. Fifty years ago, the race problem did not refer exclusively to the black descendants of the slaves, then mostly concentrated in the South. Many Americans, it was true, had come to consider the Negro a separate and inferior kind of being, biologically distinct and incapable of merging with other humans without damage to the superior stocks. In the second half of the nineteenth century theological scruples had subsided; the fatherhood of God and the brotherhood of man had receded to a remote and abstract distance; and evolutionary theory had explained that the blacks had followed such a divergent course of development as to be a species apart — hence the danger of treating them as equals.

But they were not the only ones to stand apart. On the Pacific Coast the yellow peril was the greater one. For decades since the Gold Rush, the presence of the Chinese had troubled Californians. The rice-eaters, it was argued, were unassimilable, a threat to health and morals and, by virtue of their innate inferiority, a menace to the standard of living of all other people. And no sooner were limits set upon their numbers than the Japanese, Filipinos and Hindus arrived to expand the ranks of the "Orientals." They too were separate races, therefore not equals and to be kept apart. The relocation of the Japanese-Americans after Pearl Harbor, in violation of their elementary rights as citizens, revealed the extent to which prejudice against them prevailed down until two decades ago.

Much the same kind of thinking, elsewhere, justified the position of the Red Indians, still uneasily separated on reservations. But the most numerous and seemingly the most dangerous of the alien races were not distinguished by color at all. In the streets of any great American city of 1900, the various types were readily discernible — the Italians, the Jews, the Armenians, the Swedes, the Poles and the Germans looked different and were different. A number of alternative schemes set up racial categories to describe these kinds of men as Aryans and Semites, Nordics and Mediterraneans, Latins, Slavs and Anglo-Saxons. However the lines were drawn, the purpose was to set these people apart as fully as the Negroes or Orientals.

The racist assumptions gave a new dimension to the xenophobia which had earlier troubled Americans. It was no longer, as the Know-Nothings or the American Protective Association had once thought, simply a matter of assimilating the strangers within the gates in the melting pot of a free society. These alien stocks, it was argued, were unassimilable because of fixed biological differences. And since they were also inferior they threatened to drag down "the great race" which had been responsible for creating the Republic, indeed for most of Western civilization.

Not all Americans accepted these views, just as not all wished to exclude Orientals or segregate Negroes. A persistent body of opinion held stubbornly throughout this period to the older belief in the equality of all humans and in the capacity of all to play worthy roles as citizens of the United States.

More significant than any estimate of the percentage which accepted the racist argument, however, is the fact that even those who did so nevertheless did not conceive of a single homogeneous body of whites arrayed against the blacks. Instead they viewed society as fragmented into a variety of disparate groups which could be ranked in order of their desirability and their potential for civilization. Most often, of course, the Anglo-Saxons headed the list and the Negro trailed at the bottom. But still, the essential element was a gradation of many types rather than the clear-cut distinction between blacks and whites.

The racist believed that all these breeds of humanity were unequal and would remain so for the indefinite future. The respectable science of the day taught that mankind was divided into races with fixed biological inheritances, which competed with one another in a struggle in which the fittest would survive. The social order accordingly discriminated against the inferior stocks to assure the worthy of the most desirable places in education, the economy and politics. It was absurd for the lower types to aspire to privileges above their station. Everyone suffered by such misguided efforts — witness the corruption of Reconstruction government in the South, the tyranny in China, and the anarchy in Spain and Italy. Much better for all concerned if those suited by blood for dominance were to occupy the positions of control.

The greatest danger, particularly in the United States, was the dilution of the best strains through promiscuous mixing with the lesser breeds. The latter, more animal-like by nature and accustomed to a lower standard of living, reproduced themselves more rapidly than the higher, more restrained and more decent types. It was therefore a standing problem to prevent engulfment by the inferiors. Under these circumstances the superior stocks had to guard their purity vigilantly, suppressing any base impulse toward intermarriage or miscegenation, lest the loss of strength lead ultimately to race suicide. It was a commonplace assumption that mixed breeds always lost the good qualities and perpetuated the bad of the parent stems. Social distance among these groups was therefore essential.

The tension generated by these prejudices often broke out into overt violence. Negroes were the greatest sufferers. They were the targets of bloody riots in Atlanta, Springfield, Illinois, East St. Louis, Houston, Chicago and Detroit and intermittently of lesser outbreaks elsewhere. But they were not alone thus to be assaulted; Greeks in Omaha, Italians in New Orleans, Mexicans in Los Angeles and Jews in New York also felt the shock of attacks by unruly mobs. The Klan of the 1920's was fully as concerned with Catholics and Jews as with the colored man.

The more important, although less dramatic manifestation of prejudices was discrimination. Restrictive covenants, gentlemen's agreements and informal understandings kept the most desirable residential neighborhoods pure. Hiring policies reflected racial attitudes; the best jobs were for the best-blooded. Many professional schools and some colleges adopted quotas to limit the admission of unwanted groups. Hotels, clubs and restaurants felt free to exclude clients of blemished ancestry. Some trade unions did the same.

The Negroes were the most prominent victims, not only because of their visibility but also because they were concentrated in a single region of the country, the South, where discriminatory practices were formalized into a system that had the sanction of law. What was done elsewhere sporadically and covertly could there be done consistently and openly and with the full support of the state. That made a significant difference, but one which should not obscure the fact that other people then deemed inferior suffered in the same way. Jews and Italians and Poles also knew the icy rebuff of the real estate agent and the corporate personnel manager, of the desk clerk and the headwaiter; and their children too were turned away from the medical schools and prestige colleges. In these respects, the Negro was one among many minorities, all of which labored under similar disabilities, although to different degrees.

The Negro did not stand alone. Others shared his experiences and his feelings and shared also his battle for equality. Indeed, by the 1920's, all the minorities put together formed a majority of the American population and, with their sympathizers among the older stocks, were able to effect a radical transformation of attitudes.

Between the end of the First World War and the 1950's, these Americans struggled incoherently, but largely successfully, to dissolve the old prejudice and to alter the view of race from which it emanated. The new understanding of science, the tragic events of the 1930's and 1940's and an altered political situation supplied the means for effecting the change.

After 1920, the findings of genetics, psychology, sociology and anthropology invalidated the older conception of biologically fixed races. Heredity was assigned a far less determinative role than formerly and the importance of environment seemed correspondingly greater. The most significant differences among actual human groups were now traced to cultural and social factors; and the notion of a pure race was reduced to the level of myth. Historians also began to explain the contributions to American life of Negroes and other minorities who had strengthened rather than weakened the nation.

Meanwhile the great depression set in and, before that was over, war tore across the world. Both disasters created a sense of crisis and led to a questioning of old assumptions. In the face of common dangers, the society needed for survival all the human energies it could muster; and divisive prejudices were revealed as dangerous and foolish distractions that kept America from getting the job done. Across the oceans in Germany and Japan brutal leaders pushed racism to an extreme and in their internment camps and gas chambers demonstrated the logical corollaries of

[27]

the denial of human brotherhood. Americans reacted with horror to the consequences of what had formerly seemed like innocent ideas. By 1945 the trials of fifteen hard years had created among them a feeling of solidarity and common purpose incompatible with discrimination.

The new frame of mind imbued with vitality the coalition among the minorities that had been gradually taking form since the 1920's. At first the posture was purely defensive; Negroes, Catholics, Jews and immigrants reacted to attack by joining forces. All were underprivileged and discriminated against; that was their common interest. As the years passed, these people learned that they could not protect themselves as Negroes or Jews or Italians. Their only security lay in asserting the right of all individuals to equality. Hence, the characteristic tactic of this period was to discourage or forbid discrimination on the basis of color, creed or national origin.

The combined forces of the minorities already seemed a potent political factor in 1928. They were to gain steadily in the next quarter-century. In addition, they attracted the support of many Americans who did not themselves suffer from prejudice but who responded to appeals to the creed of equality. After all, open opportunities, the free competition of talents, and the right of each man to be judged for what he was as an individual — these were concepts that reached far back in the traditions of the nation and that still evoked a response among Americans. Equality, in this sense, was attractive because it gave every person a fair chance to make of himself what he could and also because it helped identify and select those most able to serve society efficiently. Equality meant not only that every youth could aspire to be a doctor, but also that those who did not could be sure that the best qualified would be trained to practice medicine. All men thus had a stake in the principle.

The movement for equal rights therefore attracted wide followings in most parts of the country. The new labor unions which organized the mass industries in the 1930's saw its relationship to their own fight for recognition and better working conditions; and for a time it was associated with the more idealistic aspects of Franklin D. Roosevelt's New Deal and Harry Truman's Fair Deal. But civil rights commanded the approval also of such conservative leaders as Robert A. Taft and Dwight D. Eisenhower.

The campaign was consequently conducted on a broad front. It mobilized not a single group struggling for its own objectives but numerous Americans of all sorts who understood that they had a common interest in equality. Its comprehensive quality made the movement successful. One of the measures of its achievements was the subsidence of hatred, even against the Japanese-Americans who had been so harshly treated only a few years before.

Three weapons served in the course of the battle. Education clarified the basic issues and spread an awareness of the problem of the minorities. Political action aimed to secure legislation that would assist them. And litigation turned to the courts for the redress of wrongs and for relief from illegally maintained adverse conditions.

Education was effective because it emanated from a variety of sources and was cumulative in its impact. Defense agencies, representing many ethnic groups, took a hand. The NAACP, the American Jewish Committee, the Catholic Interracial Council, the Common Council for American Unity and the National Conference of Christians and Jews were but a few of the organizations that participated in arguing the case for equality and in diffusing the information on race made available by science. The foundations took an interest in the subject — not only the General Education Fund, the Garland Fund and the Rosenwald Foundation, which were specifically concerned, but also the Carnegie Corporation, which sponsored Gunnar Myrdal's monumental *An American Dilemma.* The books of Carey McWilliams and Louis Adamic stated the position against prejudice on a more popular level; and the theme of tolerance began to find a place in textbooks and in the teaching at schools and colleges. By 1945 racism had ceased to be an intellectually respectable doctrine.

Political action was far more difficult because of the complexity of American government. Generally the civil rights movement sought not only to eliminate any bias in the operations of government itself, but also to use the police power to outlaw discriminatory practices as contrary to public policy. A score of states and many more municipalities enacted fair employment, housing and education legislation of various types. But it was hardly conceivable that the South, where the Negroes were mostly disfranchised and where the other minorities were weak, would take similar action. There, the commitment to inequality, at least of the Negro, was so firmly bound into the political order that it was visionary to imagine the situation would correct itself.

Hence the resort to federal intervention. There was a valid constitutional basis for the use of national power toward this end and Reconstruction laws offered a precedent for doing so. Furthermore every President since Coolidge was, to some degree, sympathetic. The very nature of the office, responsive as it was to national rather than local needs, made its holders sensitive to the problems and the political strength of the minorities.

It was quite different in the Congress, the members of which represented local interests and depended upon local votes. The allocation of seats both in the House and in the Senate grossly favored rural at the expense of urban areas and thus deprived the minorities of influence proportionate to their numbers; and the one-party and seniority systems together with the threat of filibuster gave Southerners an effective veto on legislation of which they disapproved. Alas, the machine politicians who generally represented the Northern urban districts rarely possessed the tactical skill or ability to maneuver to break the Southern stranglehold on Congress.

The political phase of the civil rights struggle therefore involved a continuing contest between Presidents who proposed and congressmen who disposed. The long and un-availing effort to pass a federal antilynching act and the failure of FDR's "purge" of dissident congressmen showed how little progress had been made on this front by the time the United States entered the Second World War.

President Truman made a fresh start when he appointed a committee to investigate the state of civil rights in 1947. *To Secure These Rights,* the report delivered a year later, asked that the federal government assume greater leadership than in the past in bringing the country closer to its historical goals of human freedom and equality under just laws. It called for the elimination of segregation, for machinery to end discrimination in the civil service and for a federal fair employment practices act. Insofar as the President could, he implemented these recommendations. In July 1948 he ordered equality of treatment and opportunity for all persons "without regard to race, color, religion or national origin" both in the armed services and in federal civilian agencies. In these areas, integration at the stroke of his pen proceeded steadily and without difficulty. But Congress proved intransigent when he attempted to goad it into motion in matters that required legislative action. Even the evidence of popular support in Truman's reelection in 1948, despite the Dixiecrat revolt, was not enough to extricate the bills he desired from the quicksand of Capitol Hill. When he left office, the prospects for relief from this source were dim indeed.

The greatest achievements therefore were to come indirectly through litigation. The constitutional guarantees of individual liberty provided a basis for appeals to the courts that were far more effective than the cumbersome apparatus of politics.

The Bill of Rights — and notably the Fifth Amendment — had restrained Congress from depriving any person "of life, liberty, or property, without due process of law" or from interfering with the free exercise of religion. This was an adequate barrier against discrimination under cover of federal law.

But it had not impeded the states from using their power to penalize the members of minority groups. Since Reconstruction the courts had taken a lax view of the terms of the Fourteenth Amendment which forbade the states from abridging the privileges or immunities of any citizen or from depriving any person of life, liberty or property without due process of law. The Supreme Court had been inclined to place few restraints upon the states so long as their actions — no matter how prejudiced or injurious to personal rights — were procedurally correct. The only exceptions had come from marked judicial solicitude about measures that affected property rights.

Between 1923 and 1925, however, three cases reversed the trend. Two of them ruled that statutes forbidding the teaching of foreign languages or the operation of private and parochial schools were unconstitutional because they interfered with the liberty of parents to direct the education of their children. These decisions not only struck down laws directed at minorities, but they laid the groundwork for the principle that states were answerable in the federal courts for such violations of individual rights. The third case, *Gitlow* v. *New York,* made the principle explicit. It ruled that the Fourteenth Amendment made binding upon the states the same restraints that the Bill of Rights placed upon the federal government.

In the next two decades the Supreme Court cautiously explored the implications in a succession of cases involving free speech, religious liberty and civil rights in the effort to establish a line between legitimate state actions and those which improperly interfered with personal liberty. In the course of doing so, the Court held that laws which penalized an individual because of his ethnic identity violated his rights. In declaring restrictive real estate covenants unenforceable in 1948, it even ruled that the state could not lend its authority to support private agreements to discriminate. In a case involving Japanese-Americans in 1943, the Supreme Court pointed out: "Distinctions between citizens solely because of their ancestry are by their very nature odious to a free people whose institutions are founded upon the doctrine of equality."

These decisions, which dealt with the problems of a variety of types of underprivileged Americans, in time focused upon the situation of the Negro. The developing perception of the relevance of the Bill of Rights to the minorities brought the Court squarely up against the problems of segregation. Did the Southern Jim Crow system create such odious distinctions based upon ancestry? *Plessy* v. *Ferguson*, the ruling case since 1896, had acknowledged that the object of the Fourteenth Amendment was "undoubtedly to enforce the absolute equality of the two races before the law." But, the judges then had gone on to say, "it could not have been intended to abolish distinctions based on color." Laws permitting or even requiring the separation of blacks and whites did "not necessarily imply the inferiority of either race to the other." Therein the judges had chosen to disregard actualities. In refusing to acknowledge that the intent of the legislatures which enacted the Jim Crow laws was precisely to establish the inferiority of the Negro, they created a legal fiction upon which they erected the concept of separate but equal as the criterion of constitutionality.

When the Supreme Court returned to this issue in the 1930's and 1940's, therefore, it did not deal with segregation as such, but with equality. The suits brought to it by the NAACP were designed "to force *equal* if separate accommodations for Negroes as well as whites." That is, they did not aim to compel the South to surrender segregation but to provide the equality it professed it provided. A long line of cases before 1954 dealt with discrimination in voting, in education, in interstate and intrastate travel, in recreation and in the selection of juries. Invariably the Court found that the facilities provided Negroes were not in fact equivalent to those for whites; and invariably the decisions made it clear that segregation could be countenanced only if the accommodations were made equal. The judges had not set out to eliminate separateness from the Southern social system; but it was their duty to pass upon the extent to which that system treated all individuals equally, and they acted upon the facts.

The Southern states complied with specific rulings. But they did not accept the implications of the law in good faith. Perhaps they could not have; it would have been hopelessly expensive to create two parallel and equal sets of institutions. But neither were the white Southerners willing to take the alternative course of liquidating segregation; political leaders who for decades had pandered to popular race prejudice could not bring themselves now to acknowledge their error. Instead they clung to the unconstitutional policy, yielding only so much as each case demanded. The courts and the country therefore faced the prospect of an endless chain of litigation, debilitating to all its participants and irritating the wounded feelings of all concerned.

The truth was that the doctrine of separate but equal was already dead in 1954. It was dead but it would not lie down until the Supreme Court in *Brown* v. *Board of Education* buried it. There was little that was unexpected in that decision. While it frowned upon segregation because of the feelings of inferiority it generated, the ruling rested upon the incontestable finding that there patently never had been equality under the dual system. Sixty years of experience since *Plessy* v. *Ferguson* had made that amply clear. And without equality segregation had to go. What was novel in the Brown case was its sweeping character that went beyond the issue at hand and the notice by the Court that it would require a general program of desegregation to implement the constitutional principle.

The decision of 1954 was thus only the culmination of a long process that in the end focused on the rights of the Negro but that had proceeded through a concern about the disabilities of all minorities and that had taken its start from the rights the constitution guaranteed to all individuals. The roster of organizations which filed *amicus* briefs in support of the NAACP cases between 1938 and 1954 is eloquent evidence: American Association for the United

Nations, American Civil Liberties Union, American Federation of Labor, American Federation of Teachers, American Indian Citizens League, American Jewish Committee, American Jewish Congress, American Unitarian Association, American Veterans Committee, Civil Liberties Department of Grand Lodge of Elks, Civil Rights Defense Union, Congress of Industrial Organizations, General Council of Congregational Christian Churches, Human Rights Commission of the Protestant Council of the City of New York, Japanese-American Citizens League, National Bar Association, National Lawyers Guild, Non-Sectarian Anti-Nazi League, Workers Defense League. All these groups and others felt as Americans that they had something to gain from the outcome.

In that respect, the nature of the decision in the Brown case and the line of precedent upon which it rested were particularly significant. The ruling was essentially negative, not positive. It did not enjoin any particular action; rather it forbade behavior by the states that infringed upon rights guaranteed by the Constitution. And the rights it protected were not those of groups but of individuals. It did not say that Negroes or whites had a claim to one kind of privilege or another, but only that the state could not deny equal treatment to any man because of his race. Therein it followed the soundest traditions of the Republic.

It was not through failure of the Court that the consequences fell short of expectations. The decision laid a basis upon which a healthy adjustment could have been, and perhaps still can be, worked out. But it was not the duty of the Court to secure compliance with its ruling. The inadequate results of the decade that followed were due to hesitation and resistance on the part of others.

IV

▣▣▣▣

Hesitation and Resistance

THE decision in the Brown case evoked little immediate adverse response. The Negroes and their supporters hailed it as a landmark — the point at which the nation turned toward the social revolution of equality. Some Southern spokesmen deplored the ruling but not in the inflammatory tones that would become familiar later. Neither the tactics nor the need for resistance were yet clear.

The Southern politicians in 1954 were, after all, chastened. In 1948 Harry Truman had forced a strong civil rights plank onto the Democratic platform and had been resoundingly reelected; the Dixiecrat revolt then had boomeranged, for it had revealed that the presidential candidate was not totally dependent upon support from the solid South. Four years later the rebels had come disconsolately back into camp; but Senator Russell, their favorite, had made no headway in the convention and they were forced to swallow both an offensive civil rights plank and a liberal champion, Adlai Stevenson. Nor could they find much consolation in the party defeat of that year, for Dwight D. Eisenhower also bore with him into the White House a liberal reputation that gave no grounds for the belief that he would champion inequality. However they might dislike the prospect of desegregation, Southerners seemed in no position to do much about the decision.

The fact that this was but one of a long line of adverse rulings also softened its impact. The states were, by then, hardened to rebuffs at the hands of the Supreme Court. For almost three decades they had grown accustomed to having their laws declared unconstitutional; this action did not seem more calamitous than its predecessors. The heavens had not fallen then; they would not now.

Many Southerners had grown accustomed to squirming out of their dilemma by the magic of dual time perspectives. Privately and in their hearts they knew that segregation could not permanently be maintained; as late as 1956 fully 55 per cent of the whites in the region told pollsters that a day would come when the facilities of the two races would be totally integrated. But that consciousness did not impel the good citizen of the South to do anything either to further or to prepare for what was bound to happen. Since what was inevitable was undesirable, he evaded the issue by persuading himself that gallant if futile resistance would postpone the day. The evil future was on its way — but not now.

This frame of mind made it possible to absorb the Court decision without excessive shock. It was a long but not unusual step toward what was bound to happen but what was still remote in time.

And, indeed, nothing much did happen at once. The decision of 1954 had made no provisions for implementation but had asked the interested attorneys to suggest how and when to realize the principle it established. A year later, the Court ordered "a prompt and reasonable start" toward compliance, although it recognized that additional time might be required and that solutions might vary according to local circumstances. It merely directed the federal district courts to supervise the process by which children were to be admitted to public schools on "a racially nondiscriminatory basis with all deliberate speed."

The Court was moved to caution by the consideration that education was historically a local function operated under state auspices, and by the belief that no single blueprint could apply to the diverse conditions throughout the country. Its order was to eliminate discrimination — not to impose everywhere one particular system of education or another. Furthermore, it was concerned — perhaps too much so — about the administrative difficulties involved in the change and feared to require a radical disruption of existing plants, transportation arrangements, personnel and transfer policies.

Events proved that its caution was unnecessary and damaging. The largest cities, where the problems might have been expected to be greatest but which accepted the decision in good faith, made the change speedily and without difficulty. Baltimore, Louisville, St. Louis, Washington and Wilmington complied promptly and effectively as did most school districts in West Virginia and Missouri. In areas where compliance was prompt, the decision evoked the least opposition. However firm the previous tradition of separateness there had been, the pattern of segregation simply fell away.

No doubt, the problem was less complicated in the border states than in the Deep South. Yet Baltimore and the District of Columbia had Negro populations as dense as in most Georgia counties, and the habits of segregation had been almost as fixed in those cities as in the rural South. The certainty of integration, however, was so strong that the opposition never took shape. In Delaware, for instance, a protest movement developed too late to be effective, and collapsed.

But elsewhere, the vague injunction about all deliberate speed provided an excuse for procrastination and offered the hard-core segregationists the time to develop and mature the schemes for resistance.

In 1955 and 1956 talk in the South about the means

of circumventing the Brown decision was largely abstract and theoretical. In practice there seemed no alternative to letting the law stand as the Court interpreted it. But it was comforting to speculate about the means of defiance; and the polls showed a disconcerting decline in those years in the percentage of white Southerners in favor of the 1954 decision.

Their daydreams reached back to the pre–Civil War theorists of nullification. John C. Calhoun had erected an elaborate argument to prove that any sovereign state had a right to test the constitutionality of a federal action by nullifying it. The firmness of President Andrew Jackson had blown that conception down like a house of cards. Even in the 1830's, it was inconceivable that the nation could operate effectively if the states could thus call its duly enacted measures into question. In the century that followed, a great civil war had further narrowed the range of local power and the country had grown more unified, its sections more interdependent and regional eccentricities less tolerable. The federal government in the 1950's was not all-powerful; but the limits on its authority were set by the Constitution as interpreted by the courts, not by the states. State sovereignty was a rhetorical figure of speech that corresponded to no reality.

That did not inhibit the theorists who were not interested in reality. In the magnolia world that had never existed, but that was their ideal, it was altogether possible to endow the state with majestic sovereignty. There an act of Congress, or of the President, or of the Supreme Court did not have to command the obedience of people who considered it unconstitutional; their guardian state could interpose its authority to protect them until an amendment settled the issue. The idea was entirely fanciful. Not a shred of law supported it; and it would have given any minority with power in a state legislature the right to bring orderly federal government to a halt.

Those who clutched at this straw moved into the ranks

of the White Citizens Councils. There were some efforts to revive the Klan, but that organization was so discredited as to hold few attractions for respectable people. The Councils, on the other hand, offered a means of protest to men of substance who did not wish violence or disorder, but who somehow hoped to subvert the law while still clinging to its forms and procedures. A splinter faction of activists demanded more forceful action. But the movement as a whole grew slowly, held back as it was by internal divisions and by the lack of a realistic program.

Early in September 1956 the incident in Clinton, Tennessee, showed how fluid the situation still was. That little town had carefully prepared to integrate by enrolling eight Negro students in its high school. The service clubs, civic organizations and churches had laid the groundwork so that people were ready for the step; and there was no sign of trouble until the appearance on the scene of Frederick John Kasper, an agitator from New York and a recent convert to the doctrines of white supremacy and of fascism. The good citizens of Clinton refused to pay him any attention and warned him away; but he found a hearing in the surrounding mining villages and farms which supplied part of the student body of the high school. These depressed folk — isolated, suspicious, fearful — could be stirred to anger; they drifted down to town and became the mob that picketed the school in the week of its opening and that day by day grew larger and more threatening.

The reaction of the responsible citizens staved off a disaster. Authorized to do so by the mayor and the Common Council, Leo Grant, Jr., a local attorney, recruited and armed an emergency posse. In the showdown, these fifty men faced and dispersed a howling crowd of almost a thousand; the school remained integrated; and Kasper was jailed for inciting to riot. At this stage the demand for resistance to the Supreme Court's decision was still led by vagrant demagogues and drew support from the most marginal social elements; and it could still be contained by the determination and good will of responsible citizens.

The tragedy was that the sense of determination which saved the day in Clinton was already ebbing in 1956. Through much of that year political considerations and intellectual vacillation in both the North and the South were creating a mood of moderation, a disposition not to hasten the pace of integration if to do so would cause dissension. Hesitation at that critical moment gave the segregationists time to gather strength, to prepare a line of defense and to muster the resources for resistance.

Political factors had, from the start, been important in the formation of the White Citizens Councils. The racial issue had not been the only — and perhaps not even the most significant — consideration in the maneuvers of these groups in 1955 and 1956. Everywhere the problem had been confused by struggles for local political control in the wake of the economic and social changes that had transformed the South since 1945. In many places, entirely apart from the very real emotions generated by the leveling of racial barriers, the question was an instrument in the fight for political power.

Complicated jockeying for position within the national Democratic party also contributed to the uncertainties of 1956. President Eisenhower's illness the previous fall had in effect advanced the presidential election by a whole year. In the months that followed, doubts about the President's health dominated the nation's political thinking. In the Democratic party, and particularly in the camp of Adlai Stevenson, there was considerable confidence — in which the wish was father to the calculation — that Eisenhower would not run again. Relieved of the necessity of dealing with the magic of Ike's name, and cheered on by discontent in the farm belt, the Democrats imagined that they could readily regain their primacy of the 1930's and 1940's. It therefore seemed more important to concentrate on the nomination than upon the election. Stevenson was confident he would again be designated as candidate, but he wished to lead a united party that would be certain to win in November. To do so, he had to appease the Southerners who had bolted openly in 1948 and some of whom defected surreptitiously to the GOP in 1952.

Stevenson himself had always been a moderate. But moderation in 1952 had been located somewhere between the strong desegregationist position of Governor Mennen Williams of Michigan and the strong segregationist position of Senator Richard Russell of Georgia. Four years later, however, moderation had moved over to some point between the positions of Stevenson and Russell. The candidate presumptive therefore found it necessary to soothe Southern sensibilities, and the convention of 1956 witnessed a further retreat on the civil rights issue. The plank in the platform of that year was weaker than those of 1948 and of 1952.

By the time it became clear that Eisenhower would run and that the election would be a serious contest, it was too late to shift ground. The net result was to encourage the intransigent Southern wing of the Democratic party. The Republicans were under no pressure to take a vigorous stand and the liberal Northern Democrats were isolated by the resounding defeat of the Truman-Harriman group. Nothing in the vague platitudes uttered in the course of the campaign of 1956 was likely to arouse Southern fears that the federal government, whether Republican or Democratic, would act positively to enforce the law.

After that election, in fact, the school question seemed to recede in importance. During the winter and spring, attention focused instead on the erratic course of a new civil rights law through Congress. The actual contents of the act, vague and indecisive as they were, were less important in the long run than the achievement of getting it passed at all; and that was the result of a successful compromise arranged by the Democratic leaders of the Senate.

Control of the upper house had remained in essentially the same Southern hands for twenty years, but subtle changes had transformed the outlook of some of its leaders. A significant cleavage had developed between the representatives of the Deep South and those of the border states, including Texas. The role of the Texans was especially critical, for among them were Lyndon B. Johnson, majority leader of the Senate, and Sam Rayburn, speaker of the House.

In Texas, as in the border states, industrialization had effectively shattered the remnants of the Old South. The dominant groups in those places were above all interested in the tranquility and stability that would foster continued development; and they were disposed, even if they would not openly acknowledge the fact, to accept desegregation as a way of settling the disruptive race problems once and for all. Lyndon Johnson and those who worked with him were also concerned with preserving the power of the Democratic party and their own place in it. They knew that their position in Congress depended upon majorities which could be secured only if Democrats were able to win in the North as well as in the South. They understood too the significance of the Republican inroads below the Mason-Dixon line in 1952 and 1956, and some of them were troubled by factional struggles in their home states. As a result they considered moderation essential to keep the party united and victorious.

In practice, their tactics were to secure the acquiescence of the Southerners to the principle of a civil rights bill while putting pressure on the Northerners to yield on every disputed detail. The jury trial provision and the abandonment of the strong enforcement clauses of Article III were the price Northern liberals paid for immobilizing the Southern die-hards and preventing a filibuster. In the early summer of 1957, the moderates seemed to have succeeded brilliantly. Senator Strom Thurmond of South

[43]

Carolina failed in the attempt to stage a filibuster, and the bill became law.

The last stand of the senator from South Carolina gave notice that the extreme segregationists were not to yield without a fight; and his effort was only the first stage of a general counterattack. As in the decade before the Civil War, the extremists of the Deep South were above all anxious to avoid isolation from the border states. That South Carolina, Georgia, Alabama, Louisiana and Mississippi alone counted for little in national affairs had been demonstrated in 1850, and again in 1948. Only association with the larger Southern grouping would enable the hard-core segregationists to make their weight felt. To them, the civil rights bill was an ominous foreshadowing of what might come, precisely because the border-state congressmen had taken an independent line. If that situation persisted, it might lead to a broad realignment in which the Deep Southerners would suffer. Hence the importance of the school issue to them. Not only was integration in the border states a threat to segregation everywhere, it was also the decisive test of whether the extremists in the Deep South would be isolated or not. Their strategy was to provoke conflict over integration that would mobilize the broadest possible range of opinion in their support. That was the meaning of Little Rock.

Little Rock was not a Deep Southern, but a border city. The percentage of Negroes in its population was smaller than that in Washington or in Baltimore. The problem of adjusting its schools to the Court decision presented no unusual difficulties. The integration plan adopted in the city was moderate, to be slowly worked out over a long period of time; indeed it was challenged in the courts by Negroes unhappy with the snail-like pace it anticipated. The public was well prepared to accept desegregation. The conflict which led ultimately to the use of federal troops arose not out of fear of integration which elsewhere in Arkansas proceeded peacefully, but out of the

[44]

desire to make political capital of the problem. This was the riposte of the extremists.

The crisis probably originated in a visit by Governor Griffin of Georgia to Governor Faubus of Arkansas, in the course of which the fear of the politicians of the Deep South that they might be isolated was undoubtedly expressed. The ambitious demagoguery of Governor Faubus brought the crisis to the boiling point. On September 4, 1957, in defiance of a federal court order, he directed the Arkansas National Guard to prevent the Negro children from entering Central High School. Every step he took thereafter showed not only lack of candor but also a determination to prevent the problem which he had created from being resolved peacefully.

In the face of such determination, the moderates were helpless. Having abjured the use of force to implement the law, President Eisenhower at first saw no means of acting at all. In the hope that moderation or conciliation would lead to a compromise, he consented to negotiate with the Governor rather than condemning him out of hand. This temperate attitude encouraged Faubus to violate the agreement to comply with the law which seems to have been reached at his meeting with the President at Newport on September 14. Then at last Eisenhower lost patience, nationalized the Arkansas Guard and ordered the army to protect the Negro children.

But the course of moderation had even then not run out. The eagerness for compromise asserted itself again at the President's conference with the governors of Maryland, North Carolina, Florida and Tennessee who had offered to mediate until once more Faubus showed that he was not to be compromised with. The President had originally announced that the conference would deal with the whole issue of integration. When the governors appeared, however, he acquiesced to having the question narrowed to that of troop withdrawal. But Eisenhower found that

[45]

the only reward of moderation was to encourage the governor of Arkansas in his intransigence.

The Little Rock incident showed clearly — what long experience with demagogues in a democracy should have revealed much earlier — that moderation works only with moderates. Extremists are ruthless and moderation (which they identify with weakness) only stimulates them to increase their demands.

Little Rock provided a trial run for the tactics of evasion that some Southern states were to perfect in the years that followed.

From Faubus, Governors Barnett of Mississippi and Wallace of Alabama learned the gambit of provoking the use of force. They could toss restraint aside on the stump, denounce the law and the courts, and in effect promise to violate the oath of office in which they swore to uphold the Constitution of the United States. They could make a mockery of the judicial process until federal force was finally used and then withdraw, martyrs conceding to tyrannical power. And when they did yield, it was on the specific issue only, without acknowledging the validity of the law in general. At great expense and at the cost of two lives, James Meredith passed through the University of Mississippi; but that did not transform Old Miss or improve the prospects of the colored people of the state for higher education.

Meanwhile, the techniques of obstruction were being perfected in many parts of the South. Prince Edward County, Virginia, closed its public schools entirely to deprive Negro children of any education. The federal courts were kept busy striking down general laws for interposition or for the diversion of public funds to private segregated schools. But it was difficult to keep up with the ingenious devices which seemed to accept integration in principle while circumventing it in practice. Paducah, Kentucky, for instance, permitted children a free choice of schools, then designated some "Negro Teacher Schools" and others "White Teacher Schools" and staffed them accordingly. Elsewhere elaborate pupil assignment systems gave local officials authority to place children for administrative reasons while purporting to set no racial requirements. Other states froze students in the schools in which they were first enrolled, again without reference to segregation.

In all these schemes, however, the presumption is that the nonobjecting child will move into a segregated school. Only the hardy rebel will face the social disapproval of demanding integration as his right; and these have necessarily been few. Yet to examine each of these devices, case by case, involves an immense load of litigation through administrative agencies, state courts and finally the federal judiciary — a prolonged process that keeps integration only a token in most of the states which have grudgingly accepted it. Ten years after the historical decision, only a tiny minority of Negroes attend integrated schools in much of the South; and the end of the struggle for their rights is not yet within sight.

The school issue is important because it is bound up with all the other Negro aspirations for equality — in employment, in standard of living, and in access to the ballot. It is also symptomatic, for the same struggle is being fought over every relic of the Jim Crow system. The right to equality of treatment in transportation, public accommodations, employment, access to the voting booths, presence on juries, and housing is withheld as long as possible, and then grudgingly yielded in the most meager form. Meanwhile sporadic acts of violence and of economic retaliation deal with those who protest and the NAACP branches are harried by local authority.

The Negro therefore has cause to fear that the road ahead stretches indefinitely into the distance and that he might be left to travel it alone.

[47]

No other minority in American history encountered this precise situation. The grievances of others had evoked protests and agitation, had been dealt with by legislation or in the courts, and then had been settled. The communities in which they lived had accommodated to them once the decision was duly made. The contrast with the Negro in the South is striking. He has secured the remedies prescribed by law, but the organized power of the state conspires to render them ineffective.

Nor is the fear of abandonment groundless. In the past decade, the federal government moved only when action was thrust upon it and its measures were minimal. The rioters whose pictures appeared in the newspapers were not brought to justice. Out-and-out segregationists still received seats on the bench. And few important figures in American politics before 1963 were willing to go beyond bland affirmation that the law of the land was to be respected to a firm statement that segregation was wrong and would have to disappear.

Meanwhile the colored man watched other men busy with other problems. The cold war, outer space, the underdeveloped countries, automation, mental health all were important enough to absorb the attention of the more fortunate Americans. Now and again Little Rock or Birmingham broke into the news and evoked shock and sympathy. After all, Americans were far more tolerant than they had been before 1945. Only now the problem of prejudice was a Negro problem and lacked for others the nagging intensity it had earlier.

It was, perhaps, indicative of the growing remoteness of the issue that the social sciences had little to say on the subject that was new; works written before 1954 still preempted the field. A few historical monographs added bits of information and flashes of insight but the most popular books and most widely used texts still radiated serene optimism when they dealt with slavery, Reconstruction or race. Significantly, the great foundations, the resources of which were more abundant than ever before, in this period sponsored only one major study that touched upon the problems of the Negro. From the perspective of many whites it seemed obvious that the decision of 1954 had settled the matter.

The Negro who knew better was left his festering fears with consequences damaging to him and to the whole society.

V

□□□□

The Isolation of the Negro

THE decision of 1954 raised expectations that ten years later were still unrealized. The psychological effects of this disappointment on the Negroes were cataclysmic. Colored parents in 1954 had grounds for hoping that their children might some day enjoy the same education as whites; in 1964 they had reason to fear that their grandchildren would still be shunted off to segregated schools. The sense of betrayal that tore at their hearts was not conducive to calm judgments about either the objectives or the tactics of the struggle ahead. The tone of discussion grew more heated and less rational as the sense of grievance grew more intense.

The Negroes did not need statistics to tell them that in this decade whoever stood still or crept forward slowly fell behind. Their own experience was eloquent enough. While other men who had also once been identified as minorities now were making rapid progress and were escaping the prejudices which had formerly weighed on all, the Negro was left to suffer alone.

The gains of some Negroes in these years were offset for the group as a whole by drastic changes in the national economy. Automation and the structural transformation of American industry radically reduced the number of unskilled jobs. The types of heavy manufacturing which, in Detroit or Chicago, had taken on large numbers of black hands once the European immigrants had stopped coming, now could expand without increasing, and sometimes while actually decreasing, the number of blue-collar employees. New handling devices even reduced the size of the forces that had once lifted and carried the goods that passed through the productive system. Such laborers, once laid off in intervals of contraction, were unlikely to be rehired when expansion resumed, for efficiency-minded enterprises often replaced them with machines.

Yet the movement of the Negroes to the cities continued almost unabated. The exacerbation of racial feelings in the rural South left the younger and more energetic itching to leave; and, in any case, there was less for them to do on the land. The backbreaking, unremunerative toil of the migrant laborer was certainly unattractive and no other branch of agriculture needed the services of the unskilled. Cotton continued to shift westward and everywhere larger units and the use of machines diminished the chances for advantageous work. However slight were the opportunities of town, they were better than those on the farm.

The new places, created by the expansion of an economy of great abundance, demanded training. The plants that dismissed blue-collar workers often at the same time increased the size of their white-collar staffs. The need for clerks, secretaries, technicians, engineers and administrative personnel swelled as that for unskilled hands shrank. The dynamic new branches of manufacturing, such as chemicals and electronics, were particularly likely to be organized in the new form. Only the traditionally depressed service trades were relatively unaffected.

The reshuffling of opportunities thus compounded the educational deficiencies of the Negro. The well-paying jobs went to people with degrees or to those who had access to specialized instruction. Colored men and women found it hard to escape the bitter conclusion that the greater progress of other Americans in this decade reflected not greater merit but the unfair handicaps which condemned

[51]

the blacks to inferior, segregated schools. The Negroes began to envision the issue of integration as a contest for advantage — their children against the whites'.

Relationships with the trade unions fell into the same context. The only group of laborers able to withstand the impact of mechanization were those who possessed both the skill and the organization to impose their own terms upon employers. Well-entrenched crafts in the building trades, on the railroads and in printing plants got increased paychecks, shorter hours, and better working conditions as the price of consent to innovations. Some of these unions had long excluded Negroes by "lily-white" constitutional provisions; others achieved the same result informally, and persisted in the practice despite the pronouncements of the AFL–CIO and the efforts of the American Negro Labor Committee.

The problem was complicated because, by their nature, these crafts grew only slowly in size. Admission was by apprenticeship and it was difficult to set abstract standards of who was most qualified for the limited number of places available. The common custom was to take on the children, friends or relatives of existing members, so that the societies often had an ethnic or fraternal as well as a collective-bargaining character. These features kept the Negroes out as effectively as did formal regulations.

This was an old problem. But in the decade after 1954 it acquired new dimensions as it extended into the mass industrial unions which had long been among the most vigorous champions of equality. The garment workers, for instance, had played a prominent role in the civil rights struggle, they were committed to nondiscrimination and they freely admitted colored people to membership. In the early days, of course, the newly arrived were able to do only menial jobs and, accordingly, were enlisted in the unskilled locals. But whose fault was it if such people remained where they were after years of service? The decisions about training and upgrading were made by the employer and the union representative, both white. And again the suspicion of exclusion mounted, the more galling now because these organizations professed the greatest friendship for the Negro.

Trade unions were private associations. But they enjoyed public privileges and therefore bore public responsibilities; and entirely apart from their legal obligations, they controlled the only channel, other than education, through which people of low status could rise. The fear that these organizations also were instruments for maintaining white superiority increased the sense of Negro isolation.

Whatever the causes, there was no doubt of the result; the colored man gained less from the economic growth of these years than did the whites. While his income rose, the gap between it and that of other Americans widened dishearteningly. He was the most likely to be laid off when payrolls shrank, the least likely to be hired when new openings occurred — not only, or not so much, because of prejudice but because of his lack of preparation. Unemployment statistics in Detroit, Chicago and almost every other industrial center told the same dismal story.

The residential patterns of the great cities gave graphic evidence of the growing distance between Negroes and other Americans. The first reward of relative affluence was the ability to find a commodious setting for the family life this generation deemed important. The spreading suburbs received those whose income permitted them to get away from the crowding and the social problems of the inner core of the metropolis; for the most part those who remained were the marginal and the dependent who could not afford to move. As the percentage of nonwhite residents of the central cities rose steadily after 1950, it offered visible proof to the Negroes that they were being abandoned, figuratively as well as literally. Although they might shift from worse to better slums or even to decent projects or apartments, the recollection of other peoples' neat little houses on tree-lined streets emptied their own more moderate gains of any capacity for satisfaction.

Although some individuals among them inched ahead, therefore, the Negroes as a group fell farther behind while everyone else advanced more rapidly. In their growing isolation, colored men began to distrust not only the racist who condemned them to permanent inferiority but also the liberal who seemed content to postpone equality to the remote future. The growing sense of isolation had unfortunate consequences for all Americans.

Ten years of frustration have confused both the objectives and the tactics of the civil rights struggle. To the spokesmen of the Negro the issue is deceptively simple. They are men and citizens and demand full and equal rights now. No one can dispute the validity of that goal. Only, the experience of the past decade has raised complex questions about what equality means; and about the answers to those questions there is considerable dispute and confusion.

In some areas of the South the problem retains its traditional form. In Mississippi or Alabama, equality still means access to the same treatment at the hands of the law, to the same right to the ballot, to the same education, the same housing, and the same jobs enjoyed by the white man. There the barriers to parity between blacks and whites are erected by statute and supported by the organized custom of the community. They violate the constitutional rights of the Negro and must disappear; to achieve that condition it is necessary at once to eliminate discrimination in the legal and the social systems.

What must be done in the South is apparent, however painful the doing may be. That will not solve all existing problems and will no doubt create new ones. But it is an essential first step, without which no further progress can come.

The difficulties of the future, however, have already cast

their shadow forward in the North and in some of the advanced regions below the Mason-Dixon line.

Equality under the new conditions of urban life North or South is far more complex than under the rigidly defined relationships of the Jim Crow system. Negative reaction against discrimination on the grounds of race, creed, or national origin has only limited effect in Philadelphia, New York or Chicago. There the law does not single the Negro out for special liabilities; nor is segregation imposed either by ordinances or by organized open community pressures. Yet the black man remains unequal. Entirely apart from such unacknowledged residual prejudices as may hold him back, he suffers from a different kind of separateness, one which is de facto, the result of his concentration in distinct residential districts and the product of a cycle in which lack of skill condemns him to inferior jobs, poor income, poor ghetto housing and slum schools.

The colored man arrives in the city without training or capital and must take what employment he can get. In a market in which demand for his kind of labor is low, he must take what pay is offered. Wages that do not keep pace with a rising cost of living compel him to find what shelter he can in an environment hostile to sound family life. His children receive an inferior education and are prepared only to follow the disheartened footsteps of their parents. This pattern is significant not only for the frustration it immediately causes, but also because it is likely to prevail in the South, as it does now in the North, even after legal segregation disappears.

Nowhere is the inequality from which the Negro suffers totally the result of law. The liabilities of generations of subordination are not easily eradicated, and some of them will persist even after all externally imposed burdens are removed. The obstacles that keep Northern Negroes out of desirable jobs are no longer the products of overt prejudice; more often they arise from differences in opportunity and training. The sons of existing union members have an easier time of it in securing apprenticeships in the skilled trades; the children of middle-class people do better on the tests that lead on to higher education even without the aid of discrimination.

Much can be done that has not yet been done to compensate for the handicaps that hold the disadvantaged back and prevent them from competing on an even basis for the rewards of American life. But the intensity of the past decade's struggle has focused the attention of Negroes on one cause, segregation, and on one cure, integration. They have come to consider racial separateness the root of all their difficulties and racial balance the sole solution. In arriving at that conclusion, they have paradoxically accepted the contention of the white supremacist that there is really no difference between the North and the South, that the one region does directly by law what the other does indirectly by practice.

As a result of these developments, the tactics of the civil rights movement have shifted. Far from calling for the abstention of government in racial matters or from insisting that it refrain from recognizing any distinctions of color, as they do in the South, Negroes demand in the North that the state intervene actively and positively to further equality through integration. Parity of treatment has consequently receded in importance and racial balance has become the primary objective.

The implications of the altered position emerged in New York City's experiment with "benign quotas" in municipal housing. State laws and public policy forbade discrimination in low income projects. But it was difficult to maintain a mixed character in these apartments because the pool of qualified whites was relatively small. To prevent the dwellings from becoming totally black the city began to favor whites in the allocation of space, although that deprived needy Negroes of decent homes. Similar devices have been used to prevent whole neighborhoods from passing the "tipping point" at which they have threatened to become all colored.

The demand for racial balance has also complicated the

school problem of Northern cities by drawing the weight of public attention to the issue of de facto desegregation. Here most schools are either preponderantly white or preponderantly black because of residential concentrations rather than because of law. Negroes have therefore demanded the active intercession of the government to redraw district lines, to locate new buildings to serve students from dissimilar neighborhoods and even to transfer children daily by bus from one part of the city to another, all in order to eliminate separateness. In their eyes the criterion of greatest importance is a balance that will reflect in each school the racial composition of the whole community.

The same set of standards evokes a demand that the labor force also mirror the make-up of the population. Since it is far from doing so now, active measures must be devised to alter the distribution of jobs and opportunities. Some Negroes call for preferential treatment, that is, for the hiring or admission to training of the black man ahead of the white. They envision some sort of quota to assure the underprivileged race of representation at all levels of employment. There have also been suggestions of the need for a kind of domestic Marshall Plan to aid the colored people. Such favoritism would be in the nature of reparations to compensate in part for the injustices of the past.

The hidden costs of these proposals are high. "Positive integration" or de facto desegregation sacrifices important communal values embedded in the neighborhood and in the ethnic institutions within which Americans have, in the past, organized their urban life. It threatens to reduce the individual to an integer to be shuffled about by authority without reference to his own preference or to the ties of family and other social groupings. There may be circumstances under which this course of action will be unavoidable; but those who advocate it show no awareness that hesitation to hasten the change may have other roots than prejudice.

Preferential treatment demands a departure from the ideal which judges individuals by their own merits rather than by their affiliations, for what they are rather than for who they are. In a democracy, such preferences always evoke the resentment of those not favored. Affiliation with one or another of the groups that coexist in the diversified society of the United States is expected to carry with it neither great advantages nor great disadvantages. Equality of opportunity is the common ground upon which all can stand. The concept of quotas, by contrast, has infinite possibilities for mischief. If it is valid for blacks and whites, why not for Catholics and Jews, or for Poles and Italians? In special circumstances, the expedient of preferential treatment may be necessary to do justice to the Negro, but its proponents have not seriously weighed its effects.

The confused and sometimes thoughtless espousal of these remedies reflects a tragic and often unrecognized ambiguity about the long-term objectives of the struggle for civil rights. De facto integration looks toward a suppression of the Negroes' identity since it assumes that any kind of separation — no matter how defined — involves elements of inferiority. It envisions a society which mixes all men so as to minimize the effects of diverse antecedents and anticipates ultimate racial balance or homogeneity in the whole population. From this point of view, all ethnic institutions carry within them the source of discrimination and therefore must go — Negro as well as white. Some spokesmen, like Louis E. Lomax, make this point explicitly and demand the disappearance of colored churches and newspapers as of all other particularistic organizations in American life. Others shy away from that conclusion out of fear of offending the whites or of raising the specter of intermarriage, yet the objective of ultimate fusion remains the basic if unmentioned goal of their efforts.

But there is also an inconsistency in the approach to civil rights by the standard of racial balance. The demand for preferential treatment tends to preserve the sense of separateness that sets the Negroes off from the rest of the population. Every effort to establish a count of how many colored children are in which schools, of how many black carpenters or steamfitters belong to the union, reinforces the sense of identity. If admission to college or medical school, election to office, or employment by a corporation were to hinge on that criterion, the effect would be the same. And, in fact, the very course of the struggle for civil rights in the past decade has strengthened the solidarity of the Negroes as nothing else has since the Civil War. They are today perhaps less likely than ever before to lose the consciousness of their separateness.

The truth is that, like other persecuted minorities, the Negroes are torn by self-hatred and pride. Reared in a culture that treats them as abnormal, they tend to absorb the white values associated with success, superior status and esteem. They cannot stifle disgust with their own shortcomings in terms of those values and they envy those who conform to the dominant ideal. Yet the Negroes know that they are not inferior, but are only made to seem so by the power of the others. Therefore they cling defensively to what sets them apart and take pride in the characteristics which cause them suffering, for only thus can they defy the unjust majority that oppresses them.

These complex feelings enter into attitudes toward the whites. Lack of intimate human contact, the inability to communicate openly and the consciousness of numerous wrongs create the loathsome stereotype into which all other competing individuals dissolve. Often the Negroes cease to perceive whites as particular people and see only The Man who cast them into slavery, who degraded them, who is the cause of their present shortcomings, and who becomes everything they wish to be and are not. The most sensitive Negroes of their generations — W. E. B. DuBois, Paul Robeson, Richard Wright and James Baldwin — have all felt these ambiguous emotions to varying degrees. The bewilderment of less self-conscious men, similarly swayed, is bound to affect their judgment of specific issues.

Other underprivileged groups also passed through the lacerating experience of hating and loving what they were not. American Jews, for instance, between 1910 and 1920, when anti-Semitism was most dangerous, simultaneously dreamed of the escape of total assimilation and were drawn toward an ethnic nationalism that rejected the despising world. The Negroes are not unusual in this respect except in the intensity of their feelings, which measures the width of the gap between them and others. But as long as this confusion persists, it will add to their frustration, for it will prevent them from clarifying long-term goals for themselves and from making clear their desires to others.

Uncertainty about ultimate objectives confuses the immediate tactics of the struggle. Reform movements necessarily attract more than their share of the eccentrics, the out-of-place, the demagogues and the frauds. Stable men more often than not are moderate. They stay at their jobs, concentrate on their personal needs and limit their vision to the affairs of the household; the unstable usually are the ones most likely to be dashing outside to notice that the house is on fire. The prophets, however correct they may be in their condemnation of what is wrong, are not likely to be dependable characters in getting the work done unless they are guided by clear and precise visions.

It is not surprising that extremists have found places in the civil rights movement. The frustrations of a decade and a century have encouraged them and the news from Mississippi and Alabama continues to do so. Ambition intrudes; the obscure minister who dreams of being another Martin Luther King or Adam Clayton Powell, has no better means at hand than a bid for the headlines through some wild statement. Various groups, competing with each other for support, are tempted to raise their bids by bold and dramatic gestures; witness the jockeying among them over the school boycott in January and February 1964. It will take time to compensate for past weaknesses of leadership.

All these problems are complicated by the haziness of the goals of equality. Men who cannot recognize what they are working for can only continue their efforts by concentrating on what they are against. But, under such circumstances, they rarely distinguish priorities or judge accurately what methods are appropriate to what occasions.

Without those judgments tactical errors crop up with distressing frequency. All issues have the same weight and are equally worth fighting for; the blackface mummer is as much an enemy as the Klansman. All prejudice seems on the same plane. There are Negroes who equate Harlem with Mississippi and the Chicago schools with those of Birmingham or who protest that they are no better off in 1963 than they were in 1863. By refusing to make distinctions about different kinds of problems, they obstruct the solution of any of them. They are inaccurate in denying the reality of any progress at all and they obscure the gradations that make any advance possible.

The same confusion complicates the choice of methods. Sit-ins and street demonstrations are the only recourse in those areas of the South which exclude the Negroes from political decisions and deprive them of the opportunity for consultation and negotiations. There they are in the position of the auto workers of 1936 whose employers refused to recognize the validity of the Wagner Act or to bargain collectively. But the same devices used in Boston, New York, Philadelphia, and Chicago reflect a misreading of the situation with unfortunate consequences. Negroes in those cities do have legitimate means of making their wants felt; on the very day when pickets attempted to sit-in the offices of the New York City Board of Education, in December 1963, the superintendent of schools was negotiating with representatives of civil rights groups. Such wildcat outbursts are as harmful as they would be in a recognized trade union. When Negroes have channels for making their influence felt and move outside them, they are likely to arouse antagonism and counterprotests that make it more difficult to attain their goals.

A misappraisal of their position also leads some to imagine that what cannot be gained by negotiation may be gained by threats. The past two years have seen increasing references to violence, both by extremists who look toward force as a last resort and by more moderate Negroes who warn that the extremists will take over if gains are not speedier. Both forget that among free men there can be no successful appeal from the ballot to the bullet and they risk the heavy cost of the loss of their case. By the same kind of perverted logic, Jews have been warned about latent or existing hostility and cautioned that the Negro will turn anti-Semitic unless his lot improves drastically, as if what cannot be gained from the growth of understanding may be attained by extortion. When the Reverend Milton A. Galamison, chairman of the New York Citywide Committee for Integrated Schools, publicly states that he would rather see the city school system destroyed than permit it to perpetuate de facto segregation, he expresses a nihilism equivalent to that of the Prince Edward County white supremacists.

The willingness to pull the whole social structure down unless it is forthwith reformed demonstrates the unhealthy focus in these ten years of the total energies of Negro communities on the single issue of integration. Other tasks have been neglected in the urgency to reach the promised land the Supreme Court revealed to them. But however important it may be to sit-in or picket, these protests alone will not develop the responsible political leadership or the social organization or the training in skills which modern American life demands.

Moreover, the same developments have clouded over the Negroes' understanding of the country of which they are a part. The more concerned they are with integration, the more likely they are to see the whole society rigidly divided into blacks and whites. Many go beyond the legitimate desire to set their own goals for the future and grow suspicious even of the whites who work with them in the civil rights movement. Few Negroes, unfortunately, are able to recognize the connection between their cause and that of such other minorities as the Mexicans and Puerto Ricans.

The Negroes who take that rigid stand are mistaken. The categories of white and black are not coherent, unified or self-contained; each encloses groups which are significantly divided from one another. Society in the United States is not made up of blacks and whites only, but also of bankers and laborers, teachers and physicians, Catholics and Methodists, Irish- and Italian-Americans, Yankees and Texans, Republicans and Democrats. It would be a tragedy to forget the way in which equality permits individuals to conduct their lives freely within these coexisting groups.

Emphasis upon the sole issue of integration would be unfortunate indeed if it were to polarize all these elements only in terms of color. The disappointments of the past decade have had some such effect among Negroes; they threaten to do the same among other Americans.

VI

□□□□

The Dilemmas of Suburbia

THE frustration of the past decade has left other Americans, like the Negroes, confused about both the destination of the civil rights movement and the best means of arriving at it. The unfortunate result has been the dilution of the sense of common purpose and a stiffening of group lines.

The solid core of white supremacists is not confused. This group has always been a minority in the country and has not changed except insofar as delays in implementing the decision of 1954 have emboldened resistance. The men bound by this attitude are mostly out of touch with a world which has rapidly passed them by. Their own horizons are bounded by the limits of the county seat within which their tribal values are formed. They are desperately frightened, ready to use any means in a hopeless cause and therefore are not likely to be persuaded by reason; but they can readily be outvoted. For the truth of the matter is that they do not count outside the states of Alabama, Mississippi, Louisiana and South Carolina, which they hold in bondage. In Georgia, their grip on power has already been loosened and elsewhere in the South they can exercise influence only when the inertia or passivity of the more moderate majority allows them to.

More significant than the intransigence of the racists

are the subtle shifts in the views of the majority of Americans who are not committed to the doctrines of white supremacy. In the North and in the South, most whites — moderately, liberally or enthusiastically — sympathize with aspirations toward equality and acknowledge the justice of the Negro's basic grievance. But they are unsure about their obligations toward him and are uncertain about the effects of change upon their own newly won security. They find themselves therefore trapped in a dilemma, the nature of which is most visible in the suburbs of the great cities.

The race problem today is most critical in the urban setting. In the rural South it retains its familiar form and elsewhere it intrudes upon agriculture only to the extent that Negroes still form part of the migrant labor force. But these are the recessive sectors of the economy and the society of the United States. On the other hand, the cities are increasingly home to the colored people and it is there they must work out an adjustment, on novel terms, with the other residents.

Affluence is relatively new to the majority in the metropolis. Many of its inhabitants can, if they wish, recall the hard days of the 1930's, and when they do, they prize the gains they have made and resent any hint of the earlier precariousness. Prosperity is due not only to the rising productivity of the whole economy but also to changes that have increased the percentage of the population in the more skilled, better rewarded types of employment.

Suburbanization is the outward manifestation of the change. The new industrial plants are islands in the chain of parking lots and highways that girdle the cities. For miles beyond there stretch the communities of homes which house the vast middle-income groups in American society, the thirty million or so families which earn between four thousand and fifteen thousand dollars a year.

These people have left the inner core of the city: they wish to escape the disorders of the tenements and apartment districts which many of them knew in their youth and they look for the cosier stability and security of smaller communities. The single-family home is the symbol of the respectability they have won or inherited and it is also the appropriate setting for the family life this generation prizes so highly. The revolution of the 1940's which has set the American birth rate rising after two decades of decline has also reoriented the interests of the young people who matured in the past quarter-century. Early marriage, the prompt appearance of the crib, and the child-centered household are characteristic.

The little house on Paradise Lane all too often rests on a shaky foundation. It is mortgaged to the hilt and its contents carry the heavy obligations of installment payments. Its owner, in the anxiety to provide the best possible nest for the family, has eagerly seized every credit opportunity and now huddles behind the shelter of twin safeguards: rising real estate prices protect the value of his home and moderate taxes limit the burden of operating costs. Naturally, he is sensitive to any development which might breach these defenses.

Such people also consider education and proper community services of preeminent importance. They themselves have little to pass on to their offspring, neither a secure status, nor a family business nor even, as in the old days, the farm. They are more likely to have installment debts and mortgages than savings or accumulated capital. From their own experience, they know the value of good schooling in opening the way to careers, and they remain actively concerned with providing their children with the best chances possible. Indeed, the quality of its educational establishment is one of the magnets which lures them to the suburb.

Another is the ability to organize there the kind of small community which will meaningfully occupy their own time and link them with the oncoming generation. The revival of religion in the decades since the war involves less often a commitment to a theological doctrine than an opportunity to center around the church or synagogue a cluster of institutions in which adults can participate and with the aid of which children can properly be reared. The strengthening of ethnic ties and traditions springs from the same avid longing for roots which will support their families against the uncertain winds of an unstable world.

The suburb then is not merely a mode of escape from the city, a means of evading the problem of strangeness, poverty, delinquency and mass education. It is that. But it is also the holding ground of positive values which are not negligible in our times. The dilemma facing its residents arises out of their desire to safeguard those values by isolating themselves from disturbing intrusions. In the 1960's such isolation may not be feasible.

Toward the Negroes, the suburbanites exhibit good will conditioned by distance. Circumstances vary widely from one part of the country to another, of course; the outskirts of Atlanta differ from those of New York or Chicago or San Francisco. But in our society the better educated, the more stable and the more prosperous are the less prejudiced; and there is a high percentage of such people in the suburb. A substantial majority of them believe in equality between the races — the moderates because it is inevitable, the liberals because it is desirable. They respond readily to the abstract pleas for brotherhood in *The Defiant Ones* and *To Kill a Mockingbird*. Some of their children join the Northern Student Movement or go down on freedom rides or help picket or sit in. They and their parents are, after all, heirs of the American creed that Gunnar Myrdal described twenty years ago; and the issues of freedom are clearer now than they were then.

But while such people recognize the justice of the Negro's grievances, they are tempted to appeal for time and to console themselves with the little steps forward, while postponing the great leaps for the future. They are not revolutionaries and prefer change to come slowly. They are gradualists and desire to step cautiously. When the black man wishes to live on their block and the black child seeks to enter their children's school, the nightmare seizes them — all those problems they had hoped to leave behind in the central city are on the way to catching up with them.

The lesser fear is of the expense involved. Those whose homes are within the municipal limits of the metropolis have already felt their budgets suffer from rising local taxes mostly, they think, for services to the poor, aid to dependent children, welfare and costly remedial educational programs. Those who live in the outer towns often had fled there precisely to escape those burdens. An increase in the size and the proximity of the colored population is ominous; in practical terms it means either a deterioration in the facilities available to the old residents and their children or else it means doing without the new car or new coat or vacation to pay the still higher taxes. And what if real estate values should plummet with the deterioration of the neighborhood?

The greater fear is of the disruption of the community. Anyone who wishes to read can learn that the presence of a Negro family does not itself depress property values; and in some places local fair housing committees try to educate the timorous. But if one comes in, others will follow and the old timers will move away. Who will then support the church and how will they get on in the PTA, the social club, the cocktail party or the tea? What, that is, will happen to the neighborhood? There are rational answers to all these questions but the fearful are rarely in a listening mood.

In some parts of the country such people will openly say "No Negroes allowed" (or indeed devise rating scales to keep this and other minorities out). Elsewhere covert measures provide a defense — restrictive covenants, gentlemen's agreements, informal understandings to preserve the character of the family in its home, in its community. These arrangements are the most tenuous in marginal districts, where the residents are the least secure and where low property values create the greatest exposure to invasion. There resistance can lead to open hostility and even violence to stave off the coming of the blacks. Not that the rock throwers or midnight phoners are prejudiced! But why don't those others stay with their own kind? Impatience with the Negro's haste and concern about their own status similarly affects the judgment of these people about de facto segregation, positive integration and fair employment practices.

Since all but the doughtiest of the whites disclaim any ill will toward the colored people and profess a firm belief in equality, they are given to feelings of guilt about the discrepancy between their ideals and practices. But they are most likely to recognize those sentiments only when the blame is not too immediate or too personal. Hence they sympathize deeply and sincerely when the distressing news comes from Mississippi or Alabama; and they absorb the rebukes of James Baldwin or Whitney Young masochistically or are inspired by Martin Luther King's injunctions to love one another. But the impassioned rhetoric suggests no feasible program and is a substitute for action rather than a goad to it. Meanwhile some suburbanites have begun to organize themselves into parents' and taxpayers' associations to resist what they consider the Negro's unwarranted aggressiveness. And as time passes, even some liberals become accustomed to the egalitarian castigations; their attitudes harden; and they come to believe that the familiar pain will be always with them.

The dilemma is most acute for those whites who were formerly themselves members of minorities and therefore allies of the Negro. They are completely in favor of equality and know the evils of prejudice and discrimination. Their organizations, such as the American Jewish Congress and the Roman Catholic Church, participate actively in the civil rights movements; and their ministers, priests and rabbis tell them that hatred is Satan's weapon. Yet signs of tension nevertheless show beneath the surface in the behavior and attitudes of individuals.

The children and the grandchildren of the immigrants, now second or third or fourth generation, are completely American. They no longer suffer as their parents once did by being Catholics or Jews or by bearing Italian or Greek or Polish names. The more prosperous have escaped to the suburbs and have settled down into the respectable round of middle-class life. Their fight is over; they wish to enjoy the fruits of victory.

Such people retain a general commitment to equality, but they do not quite understand the Negro situation. They themselves succeeded once opportunities opened to them. Why should not colored men and women do the same? In practice, the demands for de facto desegregation threaten the education of their own children who would be compelled by schemes for racial balance to share their classrooms with boys and girls from the slums or who might even be compelled to travel into the slums to school. The suburban family resents especially the suggestion of preferential treatment. It interprets equality as an open chance for all individuals to compete for admission to a good college; and often the qualified Negro already appears to have the easier time of it. He seems to be claiming more than his legitimate share at the expense of others. These misunderstandings increase the distance between the best intentioned blacks and whites in our society.

In February 1963 the editor of *Commentary*, the distinguished publication of the American Jewish Committee, addressed himself to the Negro problem in a candid and revealing article. Self-analysis revealed a latent but permanent hostility that went back to a traumatic experience of early boyhood and that left him still feeling hatred for Negroes — insane, disgusting, violent, but ineradicable loathing for their blackness.

Norman Podhoretz in that article projects his own emotions to all whites "who are all sick in their feelings about

Negroes" and suspects of self-deception those who claim to have no such feelings. Therefore the race problem is insoluble. Equality will not come without integration and integration cannot come until color disappears as a fact of consciousness. This hope will not be realized "unless color does *in fact* disappear; and that means not integration, it means assimilation, it means — let the brutal word come out — miscegenation." But since "there are even greater barriers to its achievement than to the achievement of integration," there is in effect no solution to the Negro problem.

The utter hopelessness of this point of view reflects the dilemma which most children and grandchildren of the former minorities prefer to leave unrecognized. In the correspondence which ensued, some readers dissented but a considerable number felt it summed up "a state of mind with regard to the Negro felt by more people than care to admit it." And there is disconcerting evidence that the same attitude is not uncommon among other ethnic groups as well. In Detroit, for instance, more Catholics than Protestants resist integrated housing although the former are mostly descendants of immigrants and many of the latter are of Southern origin.

A subsequent issue of *Commentary* carried a less noticed, but as significant, anonymous article entitled "Reilly and I." Its author describes the tribulations of a second-generation suburban Jew in his contacts with an Irish neighbor. Here too the difficulties of coexistence are ascribed to an ineradicable "general ill will in men toward otherness" and the prospects of a permanent peaceful accommodation are painted in gloomy tones indeed. But here color is not the source of conflict and the special problems created by the peculiarities of the Negro situation do not intrude. The prejudice and pain arise from the contact with *any* others; and the implied solution is withdrawal to the security of isolation among one's own kind.

In both articles the noteworthy feature is the failure of empathy. Neither author understands — or sees any reason why he should understand — how and why his antagonists feel as they do. Each looks inwardly at his own emotions without taking account of the fears and anger that move the colored boys or Reilly.

These expressions of doubt are, as yet, unusual either because they are not widespread or because of a reluctance to voice them. But in either case they are evidence of an ominous separateness of experience beneath the placid tolerance of suburbia. Those who have created the little islands of security for themselves cannot quite forget the existence of the underprivileged masses left in the cities; but they have lost contact. Life in Utopia Plains dulls the awareness of what discrimination means and nurtures a mild contentment with the status quo. Equality remains a valid ideal; but the strident Negro demand for integration brings the outside world too close for comfort. In this atmosphere the minority coalition of the past withers and loses relevance. Lincoln's exhortation — that "in giving freedom to the slave we assure freedom to the free" — is forgotten; and the common interest of all men in equality becomes an empty slogan. If the suburban attitudes persist and spread, the gap between possessing whites and dispossessed Negroes may deepen until it becomes unbridgeable.

VII

The New Racism

ONLY the most pessimistic Americans, in 1954, could have imagined that the distance between Negroes and whites would widen in the decade to come, despite prosperity and despite the gains of some colored people. Only the most cynical or the most foresighted could have foreseen that these circumstances would give racism an ominous new birth. Yet that divisive doctrine is once more finding audiences, although it is now put in a new form. For the moment the idea receives its most attentive hearing from extremists, black and white; but a disconcerting number of moderates are beginning to cock their ears, even if they are not quite ready to listen.

The old conception of mankind fragmented into a multitude of distinctive and unequal races has faded away. Even the most obdurate racist is no longer eager to argue the inferiority of *all* to the Nordics. In 1956, for instance, one such writer praised the "pride of race which all great peoples have — the Chinese, the Japanese, the Arabs, the Jews" with a comprehensiveness that would have dismayed his predecessors of the 1920's who were obsessed with the yellow and the Semitic perils.

The old faith has given way to a new belief which recognizes but a single inferior race, the Negro, and but a single unpassable line, that created by the color of the

[73]

black man's skin. Carleton Putnam's *Race and Reason* (1961), endorsed by the White Citizens Councils as well as Senators Byrd, Russell and Thurmond, puts the dogma "in a nutshell" (where, no doubt, it belongs): "A gullible, trusting nation has been misled by various minority groups . . . into believing that Negroes have an inborn capacity for Western civilization equal to the white race. . . . The facts are that the Negro does not have the aforesaid inborn capacity and that social integration with him invariably produces deterioration."

The arguments that sustain this theory, insofar as they can be summarized logically, run as follows. Desegregation and the judicial decisions that enjoin it rest upon false egalitarian conceptions of the nature of man. The human species is divided into fixed races, set off from each other by innate biological characteristics and limited in their capacity by their gene pools. The Negro race is far removed from, and inferior to, all the others; it has never produced a civilization and has debased those with which it has had contact. "To save the South from integration," therefore, "is to begin the saving of the United States from all the manifestations of equalitarianism and cultural deterioration." Significantly, from this point of view, segregation must not only be preserved in the South but spread throughout the Union — the nation cannot remain half unfree.

It is not difficult to unravel this tangle of misconceptions. Even were these propositions true, they would not diminish the Negroes' constitutionally guaranteed right to equality before the law. The Supreme Court's unanimous decision in 1954 did not rest upon any particular psychological or anthropological theories, although it referred to them. It rested upon a solid line of legal precedent grounded in the Constitution. Separate facilities in the South were, as a matter of incontestable fact, unequal. Even were black children innately inferior, therefore, they would have the right to protection against discrimination by segregation. In mixed schools, they would simply remain at the bottom of their classes and would present no threat to the purity of the whites. One suspects that those who fear to extend the same chances to all may not be as secure in the faith in their own superiority as they say they are.

The view of race basic to Carleton Putnam's arguments is obsolete and fallacious and has not won the assent of contemporary anthropologists, geneticists, sociologists or psychologists. He has called to his support the testimony of three old-style scientists, wedded to outworn conceptions — R. Ruggles Gates of the University of London (born 1882), Henry E. Garrett of Columbia University (born 1894) and Robert Gayre, author of *Teuton and Slav* (born 1907). A good deal has happened in the sciences of man since these gentlemen did their work. But the failure to discover more recent evidence does not trouble Mr. Putnam; he explains that a massive conspiracy (in which Communism plays a part) has intimidated all American scholars and prevented them from perceiving the truth. "Where in the U. S. could a psychologist, sociologist or anthropologist find employment if he openly and unreservedly espoused the theory of the racial inequality of man?"

One need not waste much sympathy upon these timorous or shy professors, for whom there appear to be not even posts in Mississippi or Alabama. The truth is that a maturing science has refined the concept of race beyond the point at which it was taught to the class of 1924.

A race is a classification of individuals. The category is not a product of nature but of our understanding, a device by which we attempt to order the phenomena we observe. Therefore, properly speaking, we cannot ascribe traits to a race, refer for instance to Negro intelligence or Caucasoid docility; one can only describe the frequency with which intelligent or docile men appear in one population or another. Such statistical measurements can tell us something about the group; they tell us little about any given individual in the group. The incidence of dental caries may be higher in the United States than in Italy, but a native of Rome may have a toothache.

There is evidence that various human characteristics appear with different frequencies in different populations — blondness of hair, blackness of skin, blueness of eyes and shortness of stature. These features are transmitted through the genes, the pools of which are not similar in every aggregate of people. Therefore the probability that a child born to a Swede will be blond is higher than that of a child born to an Italian. In that limited sense, heredity is a factor establishing the frequency of various traits in various races.

But in dealing with the evolution of races over considerable periods of time it is necessary to keep two important qualifications in mind. First, the lines by which biological characteristics descend are not rigid or unalterable; genes are subject to mutation, and some physical traits, such as brain pan size, which were once considered entirely hereditary, have proved not to be so. Some changes have occurred, indeed in remarkably short intervals, as in the stature of Europeans. One cannot therefore assume that the ancestors of any group, centuries or millenia away, were identical with their descendants.

Furthermore, migrations over great distances were always characteristic of mankind in the historic era and in the immensely longer period before the appearance of written records. No race can therefore be assumed to be pure or free of past contact with others or localized in any particular place. The skull buried in the African mud forty thousand years ago may perfectly well have belonged to an ancestor of Michelangelo or John Milton or Carleton Putnam.

These considerations are particularly important in dealing with the Negroes. The slaves who were brought to America in the seventeenth and eighteenth centuries were already mixed in skin color as in other physical attributes. Upon arrival they began to mingle their blood with that of other Americans and they continued to do so. The evidence is all about us. Probably not fewer than thirty thousand and perhaps as many as two hundred thousand people born as Negroes are light enough to "pass" each year. They and their progeny form a considerable element of the total population. Well over four million Americans are recognizably mulattoes; and many more, whose skin color is darker, have nevertheless some degree of mixed paternity. Between 70 and 90 per cent of the men and women commonly called Negroes have at least one known white ancestor; probably not one in twenty preserves the genetic inheritance carried away from Africa. Poor Plessy who lost that famous case in 1896! Seven of his eight great-grandparents were white, although the law still considered him colored.

What sense therefore does it make to describe the Negro race as less intelligent than any other? On certain tests, the percentage of young men designated as black who scored well is smaller than the percentage of those designated as white. But the performance of white natives of Mississippi is also lower than that of natives of New York. When allowance is made for environmental variables not much is left of the disparity in either case.

It is altogether possible that the incidence of characteristics which make for superior performance is higher in the gene pool of one population than in that of another. But thus far no necessary connection has been established between such traits and any inherent racial attributes. If any such connections should be discovered they are not likely to be weighty enough to make a substantial difference between the actual Negroes and the actual whites in the United States.

Above all, even were the two races distinct and even were the genetic pool of one "superior" to that of the other, there would be no risk, but a gain, in allowing them to mingle as equals. Our leading geneticist points out, "It is only under uniform environments that genetic differences between individuals or populations would become manifest. The closer the approach to equality of opportunity in a

[77]

society, the more the observed differences between its members are likely to reflect their genetic differences. Inequality of opportunity acts, on the contrary, to hide, distort, and falsify the genetic diversity." (Theodosius Dobzhansky, *Mankind Evolving,* New Haven, 1962, page 237.)

We come finally to the capacity for building civilizations. A hundred years ago ethnologists argued bitterly about whether the Sphinx had Negroid features. Mr. Putnam still worries about the blackness or whiteness of the pharoahs and about the shade of color of the Tuaregs who ruled Timbuktu. Such foggy issues are relevant to him for upon them rests his judgment that the Negroes cannot create a civilization. Did they produce a Shakespeare or an atom bomb, a Goethe or crematoria? Did they develop free republican institutions or totalitarian Communism?

Africans did produce civilizations of their own and environmental factors are adequate to explain the differences between those and other civilizations. We may ascribe greater merit to some rather than others; being creatures of our time and place, we are likely to rank our own most highly. But whatever validity that claim may possess will be due to the humane values and the sense of brotherhood our civilization nurtured. Its proudest achievement, for almost two thousand years, has been its affirmation of universality, its belief that all men could be incorporated in it.

The racist theories fall apart at the least nudge. Indeed, it is no more necessary, in 1964, to refute those ideas than to deny the existence of phlogiston or to prove the sphericity of the earth. And when we encounter stubborn proponents of these fancies in our day and age, we may be sure that something else is troubling them.

A more candid little book gives the case away in its title: *Close That Bedroom Door* by Lambert and Patricia Schuyler.

The public debate on desegregation has dealt largely with the shadow of the issue rather than with its substance. Not states' rights or federalism or the control of education, but this other, gnawing fear — rarely expressed — lies behind the violence of the protest against the Supreme Court's decision. The dread lest desegregation open the way to a contaminating race mixture is the fundamental anxiety that troubles many white Southerners.

It may be fruitless to argue details with the victim in the grip of a nightmare. He will not be convinced that his views of race are false, or that his understanding of history is faulty. The images that rouse his anxiety, illusory though they be, have their own reality and will not disappear through the simple demonstration of their irrationality. It may help, however, to expose the nightmare for what it is: the figment of a mind needlessly frightened of the future.

There are no grounds for the belief that a mass intermingling of the races would everywhere follow the end of compulsory segregation. All the available evidence points to the contrary. Intermarriage has been a negligible factor in the mingling of black and white blood until now. The law forbids it in many parts of the country; and where it is legal the number of unions so consummated is small. In Northern cities, where such marriages are most likely to occur, they form only between 3 and 5 per cent of those in which Negroes are involved. Expressed in terms of the percentage of white marriages, they would make but an infinitesimal fraction. It is not thus that the strains have in the past been crossed.

Concealed in the segregationist view of intermarriage is the curious assumption that, given freedom of choice, men and women tend to select mates of the opposite race. Yet this, clearly, is a purely voluntary matter; mere propinquity forces no one into love. Marriage usually takes place among individuals of common cultural, social and religious backgrounds — even where questions of race do not intrude. The same pattern is likely to continue after as before desegregation.

The obsession with the unreal dangers of intermarriage has obscured the true source of race mixture in the past and in the present. The white ancestors of the mulattoes and of the Negroes of varying degrees of lightness of skin were not married to blacks. These are the progeny of relationships outside wedlock; miscegenation under these terms was the direct product of the inferior status of Negro women. Whatever has tended to increase that inferior status has increased the rate of miscegenation. Whatever diminishes it lowers the rate. In that sense, segregation actually is indirectly more conducive to the mixture of races than is desegregation.

Through much of the nineteenth century, white men who kept black concubines suffered no loss of social esteem thereby. Until the Civil War, the women were their property, and no control limited the treatment accorded them. In many Southern states miscegenation was no crime, although intermarriage was.

Concubinage began to decline after the Civil War. It hardly exists now. It was extirpated by the liberation of the Negroes, which removed their women from the absolute power of the masters. Less formal sexual relationships between white men and black women, however, were long thereafter tolerated in many parts of the South. They were facilitated by the disorganization of Negro family life and by the simple brute fact that blacks were incapable of protecting their daughters and sisters against the aggressions of those who had once been their masters. The law and the mores were alike acquiescent. There are authentic, if scarcely credible, instances of respectable white businessmen threatening the Negro preacher who wished to strengthen the morals of the women in his flock.

Insofar as that can be measured, the incidence of interracial sexual intercourse seems also to have declined perceptibly in the last fifty years. It has fallen off precisely because the Negro now sees the prospect of leading a decent family life and because he himself has grown in self-respect and in the power to resist. The transformation in the general conception of what the law and the practices of society owe him is the most important element in that change.

The nightmarish horror of miscegenation is real. But its causes lie in the practices which have diminished the Negro's humanity and made him seem an inferior being. Only when those are purged will the deep prejudice that feeds the new racism cease to poison our dreams.

The counterparts of the white racists among the Negroes are the Black Muslims. Thousands of members of the Black Nation of Islam also accept the premise of an ineradicable difference between themselves and the whites and look toward a future of permanent and total separateness.

The quest for roots and for an identity early turned the thoughts of some Negroes back to Africa, in the hope that they could disentangle themselves once and for all from a degrading relationship. Pride and the hatred of the whites nurtured a mystique about the ancestral continent which grew more intense as the new states there gained independence. Alternatively, other colored people dreamed of geographic or social secession within the borders of the United States. These schemes are unfeasible not only because of their cost and inefficiency but also because the Negroes are Americans and not Africans; they are destined to be a part of the nation, not apart from it. Black nationalism is significant only insofar as it reveals the hurt from which these men suffer and only insofar as it reflects the emergence of racist concepts analogous to, although the inverse of, those of the white supremacists.

The Black Muslim movement had its origins about a half-century ago in the Moorish Science Temples established in various American cities by the Prophet Timothy Drew, who informed his followers that they were Asiatics about to take control of the world away from the whites who were doomed to destruction. A little later, black nationalism found expression in Marcus Garvey's Universal Negro Improvement Association which also preached pride

[81]

of race and permanent hostility. Both groups collapsed after a few years.

Early in the 1930's some of their followers in Detroit were attracted by the teachings of Dr. Fard, a shadowy figure who taught that the one true God, Allah, had selected the Negroes for a great role in history. Among his converts was Elijah Poole, who took the name of Elijah Muhammad and assumed control in 1934. The movement long remained weak, however, with far less influence than that of Father Divine, whose doctrines were completely opposite in their rejection of the color line.

Only in the last decade have the Black Muslims gained attention and strength, and they have done so by capitalizing on the disappointments of the Negro efforts to achieve equality. The same fuel that fed the racism of the whites also fed that of the blacks.

These Muslims believe that the black man is the original man, created in the image of Allah the Supreme Being. The whites are not really men at all, but devils made by a different God; and they are doomed to destruction in the not far distant future. Therefore it is necessary that the Negroes keep their identity. *"Be Yourself"* is the first commandment. "Allah has not come to bring love and peace between us and the devils, but rather to separate" the superior race from its Caucasian enemies.

Equality is therefore, like Christianity, a sham, a device by which the devils blind those they exploit to their own true interests. Integration is but a "hypocritical trick" that lures the Negro ever deeper into the American hell. Indeed the liberals who profess a concern for equality are worse than the old masters who "were wolves, and they didn't hide the fact that they were wolves." The white man with whom colored people now deal "is a fox, but he's no better than the wolf. Only he's better in his ability to lull the Negroes to sleep, and he'll do that as long as they listen to Doctor Martin Luther King."

The complete disintegration of the white world, so they preach, is imminent and inevitable. Anyone who integrates with it must share in its doom. The Negro must stand apart in every way possible; to Muhammad intermarriage is as loathsome as to Carleton Putnam and social intermingling scarcely less so.

On the rational plane, the arguments of the black racist are as easy to refute as those of the white. The concept of race is fallacious and the ascription of traits is delusive. The history is all wrong and the theology is fanciful and shot through with contradictions. But as in the case of the whites, the symptoms are none the less significant as warnings of the separateness that threatens to divide the nation. These ideas are the straws at which men grasp to sustain them as they toss amidst changes they are unwilling to confront. The tragedy is that the illusion of support prevents them from dealing with their real problems and will, in the end, betray them into still greater difficulties.

Neither the followers of Carleton Putnam nor those of Elijah Muhammad represent more than a tiny minority of Americans. Yet each has wider circles of sympathizers who shrink from the extreme racist position but are attracted by its easy explanations. The influence of most Christian churches runs counter to any denial of human brotherhood; the traditions of the country encourage the faith in the adaptive power of free institutions; and the role of the United States in world affairs inhibits the expression of views that would offend the colored majority outside its borders. Still one cannot be casual in the certainty that these restraints will always be effective.

There are signs that racist notions have become attractive under the pressure of such tensions as the past decade has created. Not a few readers approved of Carleton Coon's *Origins of Races* (1962), an old-fashioned head-measuring analysis which showed, on the basis of fragmentary evidence, that the Negro had entered upon the process of evolution later than other men. Although the author himself treated races not as abstract types but as

Mendelian populations that change in time and although he disclaimed any intention of furthering the racist argument, still those sophisticated nuances were not adequately noted and it was consoling to think that there might be a basis in what happened forty thousand years ago for today's inequities.

By the same token, the wild statements of Minister Malcolm X, the Black Muslim spokesman, titillate respectable Negroes who do not accept his doctrines or join his movement. A grudging respect for the Nation of Islam discounts its eccentricities and emphasizes its race pride, its morale and its boldness in rejecting the whites. The sight of the upstanding Youth of Islam, disciplined, powerful and obedient, arouses admiration as if it were a fine thing some day to have black storm troopers equivalent to the white. There is a picking over of the pages of history to cull credit for the race, as if that were needed to justify its present demand for equality. And there is a growing insensitivity to the sentiments of others that matches that of the white supremacist. The chauvinism of color thus spreads on both sides of a serious fissure in the society and can have damaging consequences for the future.

VIII

🔲🔲🔲🔲

This Momentous Question

"THIS momentous question, like a fire-bell in the night, awakened and filled me with terror. I considered it at once as the knell of the Union. It is hushed, indeed, for the moment. But this is a reprieve only . . . We have the wolf by the ears, and we can neither hold him, nor safely let him go." Thus wrote Thomas Jefferson. The year was 1820, when the question of the statehood of Missouri had turned men's attention to the anomalous status of slavery in the Republic. The Civil War was forty years away. But the author of the Declaration of Independence already foresaw that the sacrifices "by the generation of 1776, to acquire self-government and happiness" for their country would "be thrown away by the unwise and unworthy passions of their sons," and his only consolation was that he would not live to weep over it.

History moves more swiftly in our day. We may not have as much time to deal with our momentous question as Jefferson's generation and that which followed had to deal with theirs. And the penalty of our failure may be greater. Our society is more volatile than theirs was; and beyond our borders we compete now not with a decrepit Holy Alliance but with a vigorous antagonist, armed with a modern ideology attractive to men who should be our friends.

At best, it will be difficult to compensate for the procrastination of a crucial decade; the damage may discount the value of the genuine gains of the period. This delay, after all, has come atop those of the ninety years since emancipation. It will take a clear perception of the vital issues on the part of both Negroes and whites to halt the threatening deterioration. But one thing is certain: the situation will not remain stable; it will change for the worse or the better.

What Should Not Happen. In the South, more years go by with token victories the only outcome of the ceaseless battle. A few more colored individuals enter the white schools; they are tolerated because the normal experience of the mass of Negroes remains channeled within segregated institutions. For the sake of display, of public relations or of compliance with the law, handfuls of colored employees find places on plant payrolls, although this does little to mitigate the general hardships from which the group suffers. A few more voters qualify for the ballot but political power remains intact. The gap between the races widens. Meanwhile investors have lost interest in putting capital into the region; the pace of industrialization slackens; and everyone suffers from the failure of incomes to rise.

The Negroes lose heart. The militant minority finds its power to demonstrate sapped by lack of results; it flashes into occasional outbursts of violence and is suppressed. The majority grows apathetic and retaliates for its sufferings by covert acts of lawlessness; in a divided society detection is difficult, for Negroes have no interest in enforcing an order to which they do not consent; and the federal courts will reverse convictions handed down by juries on which colored men do not serve. The shotguns come out as whites take matters into their own hands; and, in the ensuing sporadic guerrilla warfare, republican government dies.

In the North the Negroes burn with resentment that

strengthens the sense of solidarity with their unredeemed brethren. Bands of young men go southward — at first to picket, to sit in or to freedom ride. They are beaten in the jails or driven away, but they come back on more desperate missions; a reverse underground railway brings aid to those who are fighting. The conflict polarizes opinion. Everyone must choose what side he is on.

The whites revolt. They are tired of being made guilty, of being pushed around. There is panic and anger in suburbia. Taxpayer groups form to control the outrageous costs; parents organize to protect the true values of education. Many, by now, are sending their children to private and parochial schools, but integrated public education is expensive and attracts the wrong kind of families and lowers real estate values. Obstructive court cases prevent the resolution of the issue and keep emotions at the fever point. These people do not become racists, but increasingly they believe that, as whites, they have a common interest in standing up to the blacks. The faith in equality does not die but loses its content and becomes a ritual incanted by moderates to justify the freezing of the status quo.

Desperation grows among the Negroes in New York and Chicago. Heightened color consciousness, suspicion of the remote non-Negroes and displacement of the anger at the Southerners who are out of reach adds strength to the extremists who raise the level of their demands for positive integration. The response is hesitant and the problem grows more intense. The number of unemployed and dependent mounts; delinquency becomes usual; rents are unpaid; housing decays; and the municipalities falter under the burden. The cities are almost all black now; the others have fled. The area in which violence is endemic and the streets unsafe spreads and most business and cultural activity is dispersed in the suburbs; only a few heavily guarded financial and administrative islands remain.

Here the police are more effective than in the South

and they manage to contain violence — for a time at least. But the capacity to make reasoned political decisions breaks down as the issue of color infuses all other local questions. The Negro minority is able to manipulate its balance of power only until it unites a substantial part of the white majority against it. Then there is impasse or repression.

At some point the federal government intervenes. Perhaps a crisis in foreign affairs forces it to impose unity; or some constitutional problem compels it to use its power; or people impatient with frustrating debate call for a decision at the top. However that action is occasioned, the outcome is a dictated settlement that stabilizes the existing situation, postpones any changes indefinitely and demonstrates the inability of democratic methods to cope with the momentous question of human equality.

Are these fears exaggerated? Every element that enters into them has already appeared in the past ten years.

It Need Not Happen. Other elements could be the basis for a different result. If the prospect in view at the moment is gloomy, a backward glance can lift the heart; there are more hopeful ways of dealing with this momentous question.

American government rests upon the conviction that free men can form and live in an orderly society. Tyrants — good or bad, reasonable or passionate — have, in the past, held no attraction for the people of the United States, who have insisted on being ruled by laws of their own making. The consent of the governed is the condition that secures order without the constant recourse to force. That consent is expressed in constitutions and in a long line of antecedent covenants that go back to the Mayflower Compact and the Charter of Virginia.

These are not dead documents. They are ratified day by day by the actions of the citizens. Without their consent the operations of government would collapse and the structure of society would fall into chaos. The draft call, the income tax form, the court injunction and the property of others are respected not so much out of fear of the policeman's stick as out of the consciousness that these are the agreed-on means by which to pursue ends common to all in an orderly way. The apparatus of enforcement exists not so much to intimidate as to assure those who wish to obey that the burden of doing so will fall impartially on everyone.

Americans resort to the power of government when they have secured agreement about common purposes; other matters they leave to voluntary effort. Religion thus remains outside the purview of the state, and diverse sects go their way without its support. This flexibility permits differences to persist and thus enables people of dissimilar antecedents to live and work together without interfering with each other's rights. But the necessary condition of their coexistence is recognition that that which is done in the name of all is done for all and with the consent of all.

In a free society people consent to be governed not out of terror but out of the awareness that they thereby serve their own best interests and because they prefer order to disorder. But to preserve that preference and that awareness they need assurance on two accounts: that they will receive the equal protection of the law and that they will have equal access to the opportunities the efforts of all make possible. To be able to work together and still to remain free, equality under the law must be the salient objective of Americans.

Clarity of understanding, recognition of the dreadful alternative, and an effort of the will make it so. North and South, the number of Negro voters increases; their voices are heard and their grievances recognized. Leaders who represent them are available for negotiation. Hope is born with an immediate rapid and dramatic improvement in the quality of education. Self-respect mounts under the stimulus of treatment as equals. Visible goals are worth working and saving for, studying and cleaning for, even worth waiting for. Skills rise and, in time, incomes. The quality of family life improves with the growing incentive to hold together and to support one another.

The large units in which modern life is organized make room for all. The city spreads over hundreds of square miles within which the people arrange themselves according to their preference and their income. For some, the primary consideration is access to the places of densest employment and to concentrations of cultural facilities; they pay their rent in impersonal apartments where no one knows or cares who lives next door. Others prize the small house and little garden of the suburb; scores of such communities exist for their accommodation. The absence of discrimination gives each family the ability to choose. Those who are happy living only with their own kind can seek out neighborhoods which are solidly Yankee or Negro or Jewish; those who do not feel the same gregariousness can move into mixed districts which offer other advantages. There will be a price for exclusiveness, of course, if the only way to avoid contact with the outsider is to move to less convenient quarters in a less convenient area than one can find elsewhere. But no one is thrust upon anyone else, for discrimination no longer gives advantages to some over others. In this respect, the urban South is very much like the urban North; the backward rural counties remain a problem, but one from which the energetic of both races can escape.

Visionary? All the elements have appeared in the past ten years.

No Promised Land — Yet. Equality among the races will not solve the great problems of American life. All the other issues with which this one is enmeshed will remain to trouble the nation. Inherited political techniques will still need adjustment to new conditions; unemployment will still be endemic to the economy; the educational system will still be inadequate to the demands made on it; and the great cities will still suffer from debilitating physical ills. Equality alone will not enable Americans to live happily ever after. But equality is the essential first step toward the position from which they will be able to attack these problems.

The Negro voter will need the education of experience. Having been deprived of his own rights for so long, he is not likely at once to set great store upon the rights of others. Having been taught to view all questions in the light of race, he will probably be tempted to vote in a bloc, to follow demagogues and to misread his own interests. In other words, he will make the same mistakes as other Americans unfamiliar with the methods of political democracy.

But the Negro will learn only after the instruments are in his hands. It makes no sense to talk to him of the right to a jury trial in Alabama where his name does not appear on the lists or to describe elections as tests of the will of the people in Mississippi where the franchise is withheld from him. He will not get to understand the dangers of bloc voting in Louisiana where the ballot described each candidate as "Caucasian" or "Negro" until the Supreme Court invalidated the practice in January 1964. He will only know the responsibilities of being a citizen by fully being one; and the longer he is made to wait the more costly it will be for the whole society. What is more, the removal of the distracting issue of his equality will, in time, permit other Americans to shed the layers of practice that now corrupt their political life — the one-party system in the South, the misrepresentation in the legislatures, and the demagoguery, which all thrive on the maintenance of his inferior status.

Unemployment is not peculiarly a problem of the Negroes. They supply far more than their share of those out of work; but the great majority of the idle are whites. The favored skin color is not much of an asset in the mining towns of West Virginia or among the mountaineers who have come down to Cincinnati and St. Louis or even among the workers laid off in Detroit or Chicago. Unemployment is partly the result of the inability of the economy to expand fast enough to absorb the three million adolescents annually added to the labor force. It is partly the result of automation and other structural changes which make the services of many workers unnecessary. Removal of the race issue will still leave the basic difficulties, but in a shape more susceptible than now to treatment through the expansion of demand, through retraining and through devices our ingenuity should uncover for the useful employment of the labor of all.

The question of segregation obscures the true problems of American education. Once we can cease to worry about whether the Negro child should sit next to the white, we shall be able to worry about the inadequate number of decent seats for either of them. The Negro 10 per cent are not the only youngsters to whom we fail to do justice; the Commissioner of Education sets at 30 per cent of the whole the number of underprivileged students — most of them white. Fear and uncertainty about the integration struggle, in many places, have scandalously delayed the reconstruction of a school plant which is aging rapidly and is yet expected to accommodate a bulging population. If ever a start is made on that task, perhaps then it will be possible to glance at a still more important matter — the purpose of education. We make do with a system which took form more than a century ago to select and train an elite minority along traditional academic lines. It is now expected to occupy the time — which the labor market no longer needs — of the whole population below the age of eighteen or twenty. The creaky apparatus staggers along, patched with old boards and held together with baling wire, for there is no time for the pause to reexamine the fundamental design. To approach that onerous assignment, it will be necessary first to stop thinking of the schools as a source of social advantage to one group or another.

The problems of housing, transportation and inadequate taxation will not vanish with the end of racial discrimination, but they will become somewhat more manageable than at present. The job of replacing dwellings long since fallen into decrepitude and of providing at the same time for the shelter of a rising population is immense and is complicated by prejudice that puts much of the burden on those least able to bear it while the more prosperous escape to the suburbs. Transit systems are inadequate because their users are unwilling or unable to pay for proper service. And the municipalities, confined by fear of the Negro (as earlier by fear of other minorities) within anachronistic political boundaries, lack the resources to undertake the needed reconstruction. A cumbrous pattern of subsidies palliates the difficulty. The suburbanite who prides himself on the low tax rate of his town also complains about the rising taxes of his state; he does not realize that he has not altogether escaped the costs of the city to which some of the state and federal levies he pays indirectly come back; in 1964, New York State alone will probably allocate a billion and a half dollars for local purposes. The abatement of prejudice and the redistribution of the urban population are first steps toward the more rational organization that would prepare municipalities to face up to their tasks.

We shall avoid disappointment if we realize how little will be gained by equality alone. We shall avoid tragedy if we realize how much will be lost without it.

The More Remote Future. Those who worry about the color of their grandchildren's grandchildren are unduly concerned. Their daughters are unlikely to take husbands outside the group lines; and no one will force them to do so, whatever the fate of integration.

Marriage, in the United States, is private and voluntary except in those states which set up racial impediments to the free choice of the partners. (Those laws are almost certainly unconstitutional although no one has yet troubled to challenge them directly.) No change in social patterns is likely soon to affect existing marriage patterns and certainly the increase in equality will not do so. On the contrary, all our data indicate that the growth of equality between the races does not increase, and may retard, the rate of intermarriage.

This is exactly what might be anticipated in view of the character of American marriage and of the factors that influence choices in it. All statistical measurements indicate that marriages are usually formed among individuals of common ethnic backgrounds which shape their personal tastes, habits and interests and their family attitudes. In some large city high schools, boys and girls of diverse antecedents mix without distinction of race, creed, or national origin. Ten years after graduation, the former students will have sorted themselves out in marriages with the partners closest to themselves in color, religion, and antecedents. This, essentially, is a process by which the family is extended across the generations; and those who enter upon it have in mind not only their own emotions but also the feelings of their parents and relatives as well as of the children who will come of it. In the absence of compelling forces to the contrary, opportunity and inclination will alike lead to marriage within some existing group.

Groups with an ethnic base are the most usual, but not the only ones in American society. People are also drawn together by mutual cultural and occupational ties. In some of these circles other shared interests may outweigh the force of common descent and provide a ground for intermarriage, particularly when the individuals involved are highly mobile, highly talented or wealthy and are thus able to free themselves of conventional restrictions. The men and women professionally engaged in sports, art, literature and entertainment, for instance, move in little worlds of their own, to some extent detached from the general experience. But the highly publicized instances of interracial marriage among these folk are not representative of the population at large.

Insofar as scholarly investigations have thrown light on the subject, they reveal that most interracial marriages involve individuals whose own family ties are weak. Generally the black man marries a white woman whose status is inferior to his own. The white man who takes a black wife is likely to be foreign-born, detached from any group of his own, and without binding social connections. A large percentage of those who enter upon such unions are divorced or widowed, people whose earlier attempts at marriage failed.

Segregation, which establishes the inferior position of the Negro and prevents him from sustaining stable personal and family relationships, actually magnifies the incentive to seek the escape of intermarriage. On the other hand, desegregation, which widens opportunities and increases the scope of equality, also strengthens the cohesion and order of Negro family life, heightens self-respect, and thus indirectly diminishes the incentives toward intermarriage. Equality too will probably remove the taboo which makes the forbidden attractive and therefore diminish the frequency of the extramarital miscegenation which has been the source of most race mixture in the past. In the longer perspective, amalgamation may or may not be desirable; we cannot make the decisions of men and women a century hence. For the moment this is not a real question and must not befog immediate issues.

One can expect, or at least hope, that in time equality will lead to greater intimacy in the social relationships among Negroes and whites. Partners in business, men who stand beside one another on the assembly line, colleagues in the laboratory will get to know one another. Their connections may extend beyond closing time to the home and they will share public accommodations of every sort. Treating each other as men rather than as stereotypes, they will be able to like or dislike one another, to

[95]

be friends or enemies, without reference to racial images.

It is improbable, however, that these desirable tendencies will wipe out or diminish the sense of ethnic identity which lends variety and meaning to much of American life. There will still be experiences that men of common antecedents will wish to share, still traditions and tastes they will seek to preserve. Equality does not weaken but strengthens ethnic groups, for it makes membership a voluntary choice which the individual assumes to satisfy his own needs rather than a role thrust upon him by the judgment of outsiders. This has been the case with others in the past; it is likely to be so also for the Negro in the future.

In the long run, our aim is not a society composed of people who are all alike but one which recognizes the individuality of each man and permits him without penalties to express the differences of his personality and his heritage in his own way. Properly speaking, therefore, not integration but equality is our genuine objective.

The Matter of Means. In terms of that objective, there is a consequential difference between Jackson, Mississippi, and New York City, between Birmingham, Alabama, and Chicago. No rhetoric should obscure the fact. In the South segregation was historically a device, deliberately built into the legal and social system, to establish and perpetuate the inferior status of the freed slave. It always was and is now incompatible with the Negroes' right to equality and it was tolerated only because of the myopia of Americans busy with other affairs. It must go, immediately and without qualification. The Barnetts and the Wallaces who wish to preserve it are an imminent danger to the survival of free institutions in every part of the United States. Their bold gestures must encounter equally bold resistance.

Some means are ready for use. The candidates in the approaching national election must unequivocally announce their support not only of legality but also of equality. The attorney general must use fully his power to aid voter registration. Judicial appointments in these states, as elsewhere, must go to men committed to the Constitution. The Northern and border state congressmen and senators of both parties must demonstrate the isolation of their colleagues from Mississippi and Alabama by resisting the temptation of convenient arrangements. National corporations that do business in the South must lead rather than trail behind public opinion. These are strenuous measures, but they will be less costly than renewed summonses to the troops.

In the Northern cities too there are all-Negro schools and all-Negro residential districts and desirable types of employment in which Negroes are not represented. But that separateness has historic origins, motives and effects which are altogether different from the segregation of the South. The ghettoes of New York, Philadelphia and Chicago were not established by law but by the adjustment — largely voluntary — of a heterogeneous population to the conditions of metropolitan life. The Irish, Germans, Italians and Yankees who peopled these cities chose, and often still choose, to live in communities of their own because they could thus best satisfy their social and cultural needs. The few Negroes who lived there before 1900 and the much larger numbers who came in after the First World War adopted the same pattern; and most of them would prefer still to follow it *if they could do so as a matter of their own choice* — that is, if those who preferred to leave could freely do so and if staying imposed on those who remained no penalties of inadequate facilities, depressed jobs or the imputation of social inferiority.

In the North, therefore, integration is not an end but a means toward an end. Equality in education, housing, employment and politics are the true goals; and genuine progress in that direction will push the problem of de

[97]

facto segregation to the background, as it has for other groups.

The inability to differentiate between the two situations complicates both. The bitter· news from Alabama and Mississippi narrows the attention of Northern Negroes to the sole issue of integration so that they cannot conceive of any other road toward equality. And conversely, the emphasis on integration lends substance to the Southern fear that complete amalgamation will be the result of any approach to equality. Yet our experience as a nation should teach the Negro that ethnic groups can retain their character and identity and still be equal. And from the same experience the Southerner should learn that equality leads not to the effacement but to the strengthening of group lines.

The distinction between integration and equality is crucial to any estimate of the means available to resolve this momentous question. If equality is the true objective toward which every American should strive, the problem in not then the same on both sides of the Mason-Dixon line. In the South inequality is still sustained by acts of government; in the North it is the product of self-interested, thoughtless or prejudiced individuals. In the South, the immediate remedy is clear but inadequate; when the legal impediments are cleared away, Atlanta and New Orleans will be in the situation of New York and Chicago, where the grievances of the Negro are far more complex, far less open to easy solutions and far more demanding in the choice of means of adjustment.

Anger Is No Answer. The community council of a Northern city decides to discuss The Problem. It plans a public meeting and, to present *the Negro side,* invites a representative of one of the national organizations; it does not give much thought to which one, since it assumes that all are the same. Nor does it occur to the council to consult or involve any local Negro. Consequently no black

[98]

faces appear in the audience. Later some whites mention the apathy of the colored people, unaware that the latter are seething with resentment. Such slights are the least of the sins of omission and commission that impede understanding.

Often the sins are on both sides. The matrons of Buttercup Hill make an unlovely sight to the young man on the platform. They sit before him, well groomed, spilling over with good will, and ready to exude sympathy when the horror stories come. But he knows that they would not be there were they not already persuaded, in some sense, that equality is a good thing, and he therefore restrains his impatience with their virtuous self-satisfaction. His rehearsed speech proceeds uneventfully and the question period is desultory until the slim young woman touches a sore point. She asks why *his* people cannot do more to help themselves. After all . . .

His torrential response points to the abuse of Negro maids, the restrictive practices in the suburb, the hidden prejudices of the complacent; and it concludes with the assertion that he is as much a slave in 1963 as his ancestors were in 1863. When the chairman has thanked him for his informative remarks — and we all welcome candor — the ladies leave, wondering, "Are we really in the same camp with Governor Barnett?"

Another instance: The Philadelphia Mummers have paraded on New Year's Day for almost a century, many of them in blackface competing for prizes awarded by the city. Toward the end of 1963, sensitive Negroes complain; the burnt cork is offensive and should be banned. The Mummers demur. Their rigs are ready after months of preparation; besides minstrelsy is an old tradition and not intended to insult any race; and to yield now and in this form would be to acknowledge that they are prejudiced, which they don't want to be or don't want to admit. The municipal administration vacillates and announces it cannot interfere.

The day approaches; the police are mustered. Louis Smith, aggressive regional representative of CORE, announces that Negroes will picket. "We will try with our bodies, nonviolently, to see that the parade does not go on." But he predicts that "blood will spill in the streets" and warns that an army is coming down from Harlem — "look out for the rooftops because that is the way the people of New York operate." At the last moment, the courts take a hand and, yielding to the threat of violence, forbid the blackface as a menace to the peace. Only the next election will tell how valuable the victory will be.

Boston has already had its next election. The Negro problem there is less grave than in most cities of its size because the number of colored people is smaller. But it is nonetheless a problem. A majority of the Negroes live in a single area, mostly slum, which stretches down from the South End into Roxbury; and their children attend schools in which there are practically no whites. Most of the buildings are dilapidated and there has been practically no effort to improve the quality of education there. But the elected School Committee, which administers the system, is on the defensive in the summer of 1963. Sensitive to public criticism in the face of an approaching election, it asks experts to nominate candidates from outside the city for the vacant post of superintendent and it enters into negotiations with Negroes and others to define practical measures for improving the situation.

The discussion breaks down over the use of a term. The Committee refuses to admit what is demanded of it, that the schools are de facto segregated. It is short-sighted, stubborn and dogmatic; and it evokes like responses from the civil rights groups. A sit-in spreads through its offices, tempers flare, discussion halts and the decision is left to the electorate. When the votes are counted, it appears that the Negroes have not turned out in large numbers, as their leaders demanded, but the supporters of the die-hard Committee members have. The candidates most resistant to the offensive words receive the greatest majority. Thereupon the Committee not only kills the issue but, in selecting the new superintendent, rejects the nominations of its expert consultants and appoints from within the system a man who has heretofore shown no sign of interest in change.

Everybody is to blame for the want of understanding. The young lady in the audience and the young man on the platform, the Mummers and their foes, the School Committee and its critics all, in the abstract, would accept Martin Luther King's injunction that they should love one another. Yet they stumble on the use of a term or tear into a rage about a charade, and sometimes cannot even communicate for the emotions that drown them. Commenting on the Boston election a few months later, a nationally prominent Negro leader declared that the city had become a model for white supremacists. "Governors Faubus and Wallace are sending experts here to find out how Boston does it." Whatever personal satisfaction release of his anger gave him, the statement is not only inaccurate and misleading but calculated to hinder rather than further understanding. Under these circumstances, the demand upon some that they forget their grievances and upon others that they acknowledge their guilt dissipates good will and makes every issue the occasion for an open conflict. Means that produce such results are inherently ineffective.

There is a way out for those willing to take it. The first step is recognition that The Problem is not all of a piece; there are degrees and differences and there should be priorities that will indicate which matters cannot be compromised or postponed and which can, which involve substance and which appearances. It is asking a good deal in the heated atmosphere of 1964 to ask for this first step; but it is an essential prerequisite of any further progress.

Now, as in the past, equality is the only useful criterion. What is most important and most immediate is not that which advances the interests of one group or another but that which helps all members, as individuals, to coexist.

[101]

That standard can guide men of good will to reasonable means of dealing with the current questions of employment, housing and education even though the full solution of those problems may be a distance away.

How Preferential Can Treatment Be? Every job ought to go to the applicant best qualified to perform it. That rule is fairest to all applicants and most just to those whom they will serve. In most cases, of course, a valid test of ability will uncover many persons equally capable of executing the task; dozens of pilots, for instance, are equally able to fly a commercial jet and dozens of dentists are equally able to fill a cavity. We ought not to select among them, as we all too often have, by using measurements inappropriate to their qualifications; their familiarity with Shakespeare or ability to sing or blondness, however desirable in themselves, are irrelevant to the quality of their performance. And what applies to the job itself applies also to the course of training that leads to it; the one should be as freely and as properly competitive as the other.

In the rivalry for places, most Negroes suffer from the two-fold disadvantages of their underprivileged homes. Their families rarely equip them with those marginal graces or with that body of general information which leads to high scores on intelligence and similar tests; and their backgrounds rarely supply them with the incentives to aim for the more desirable positions. As a result they do not often win out in open unaided competition, even where prejudice is not a handicap.

A quota is not the answer because it would be unfair not only to their rivals but also to their prospective clients. No one ought to be compelled to risk his life or his molars to a less qualified pilot or dentist because the airline or dental school had to have some representative of the race. But a preference for the Negro among equally qualified applicants would not be unfair since none of them has a superior claim of merit and none of them would better serve the client. And such a preference would be just, for it would recognize the greater difficulties surmounted by the colored man.

The vast majority of hiring and admittance situations are of this nature; few demand unique qualifications. It is not too much therefore to call for a reversal of attitudes among personnel and admission officers that would waive standards irrelevant to the job, that would look for as much but not more merit in the Negro as in the white and that would seek out and solicit rather than discourage applications from the underprivileged. Some firms and colleges are already doing so; many more could. More preference than this is unjust and, in actuality, unnecessary, for the Negro, under equal conditions, is capable of holding his own and has no claim to other concessions if he is not.

The Neighborhood School. The American educational system serves various functions. It transmits our culture to the young; it occupies the time of people for whom there is no place in the labor market; and it inculcates specific useful skills. It is also a screening device that sorts out the population which passes through it and directs individuals toward appropriate careers. Hence its influence upon society. Equal opportunities in the schools are the basis for equal opportunities in later life.

Communities which never were — or are no longer — burdened with a dual, separated system, have discovered the far more complex and more difficult problem of de facto segregation. The school reflects the district in which it is located and inevitably has an ethnic character paralleling that in which residence is distributed. In the large cities therefore Negro children usually find themselves still attending institutions composed preponderantly of students of their own race, even in the absence of laws that provide for segregation. This problem has already caused bitter controversy; it will cause more in the future. The advocates of racial balance demand positive steps to mix the population so that each school will contain a cross section of the whole. They argue that such an arrangement would do justice to the underprivileged and also would have the educational value of teaching all children to get along with the diversity they will encounter in later life.

The opponents of such measures have taken refuge in the neighborhood school. The school, they maintain, is more than a place of formal instruction; it is a communal center. Children will learn best close to their own homes among their own peers, when they are not confused by contact with strangers or subject to the tensions of unfamiliar surroundings. The ability of their parents to associate as a group also advances their welfare. All these functions can best be served by the neighborhood school.

The conflict between the two points of view is real. But each runs to extremes because it states the issue in terms of propaganda rather than of substance. We must penetrate beyond the slogans to see the true nature of the problem.

The case for the neighborhood school is strongest in the lower grades where boys and girls do walk to classes and where environmental conditions are most important. There the local school has a value that ought not lightly to be sacrificed. It might be a genuine hardship to start shuttling these youngsters all over town.

The situation is quite different at the upper levels of instruction, and particularly in the high school, which is, strictly speaking, not a neighborhood school at all. Except in the smallest towns, these students come by rapid transit or by bus, rarely know more than a few others outside the building and are related to each other only in the most formal and impersonal manner. They would be only slightly inconvenienced if altered district lines changed the patterns of their daily travel.

However, at no level will the simple realignment of district boundaries significantly affect the ethnic character of the schools. The percentage of Negroes in the central areas of the more important cities is already so high that it would take a rigid scheme of imposed racial quotas to create a balance. A number of test cases in New York State have shown that such efforts are probably illegal because they involve discrimination by color, although presumably on behalf of the Negro. And in any case, the recalcitrant white parent always has the last resort of a transfer to a parochial or private school or a move to the suburb.

Communal energies are therefore more properly expended on making the schools equal than on integration. Where redistricting of junior and senior high schools can contribute to a better balance, it is all to the good. But even more important is a well-planned concentration of educational resources to reduce drop-outs, to widen the horizons of the underprivileged and to make the school in the slums superior to that in the suburbs, as it should be if it is to cope with the greater problems there. Generally boards of education in the past have passively allowed real-estate promoters to make the crucial decisions. Subdividers, on their own, throw up thousands of little houses in an empty region and create a need which the board docilely fills to the neglect of the old districts. It could equally well resolve first to use its funds in Harlem or Bronzeville. Money thus expended will bring more results than it would if spent on buses. Progress in that direction may restore the attractiveness of the central city for white families and will certainly aid the black children directly.

Quotas — Benign and Others. There is a striking analogy between educational and housing policy. Efforts to engineer racial balance through benign quotas have been of dubious legality, costly and ineffective. Efforts to further equality will certainly help the underprivileged and may contribute to integration.

Public policy in many parts of the country already frowns upon bias in housing; and it is likely that continued pressure in the near future will improve the effectiveness

[105]

of enforcement provisions. Additional measures to make prejudice more costly will also help. The executive order in 1963 that barred federally supported loans for housing projects which practiced discrimination was one such step and could well lead to others if the lending agencies would cooperate.

But anything that can directly improve the dwellings of the poor, whether Negro or not, is far more important. It need not have taken a rent strike to induce the City of New York to embark upon a campaign to exterminate rats in the Harlem tenements. It should not take a social explosion to call attention to the lag between the supply and the demand for decent housing. As long as thousands of buildings are still in service that were ready for the wrecker thirty years ago, the first requisite is more space, whether it be provided by the municipalities, by private enterprises or by regulated and subsidized corporations; whether it be in the heart of the city or in the outlying districts. The rapid expansion in the supply of quarters available on a nondiscriminatory basis will at once help the Negro and, in the long run, will create a price differential that will compel those who want exclusiveness to pay for it. The means for increasing equality in housing, as in education and in employment, thus exist. Question: Is there also the will to use them?

Force to Do Good? Feebleness of the will, in the past, has raised questions about the capacity of government to act in matters which involve the deeply held prejudices of a part of the nation. Curiously, the doubts exist at the two extremes of opinion about civil rights. On the one hand, supporters of the status quo argue that the law is necessarily ineffective when it attempts to alter mores; the state cannot legislate virtue, much less love. On the other hand, some advocates of integration contend that the law is too cumbersome; its procedural loopholes tolerate or even encourage evasion and only the fear of direct action will compel the prejudiced to concede equality to their victims. Both positions are wrong.

Those infatuated with the concept of unchangeable mores are in error both about the nature of the particular customs and habits here involved and about the general efficacy of law in transforming social practices. The patterns of segregation familiar to the twentieth century are not part of the traditional way of life even of the South. They did not exist before the Civil War. Indeed, C. Vann Woodward has shown, in *The Strange Career of Jim Crow,* that they developed only toward the end of the nineteenth century as a means of maintaining the supremacy of the former masters over their former slaves. They became fixed in the relatively brief period of a decade or so. And there is no evidence that the habits of fifty or sixty years cannot be altered, given the determination and resolution to do so. In fact, the experience of Southerners who move to the North and the success of integration in the armed services show that the change can be induced with relative ease.

The function of law in the process is complex. An act of a representative legislative body not only draws upon the support of the organized power of the state; it commands respect because it also stands for the deliberate opinion of the community and formulates a code of decent behavior. The laws which are violated — like prohibition or traffic regulations — are those which the community itself does not wish enforced and which are therefore applied capriciously and haphazardly.

A civil rights bill, such as that which was submitted to Congress in the spring of 1963, may prove an empty gesture if it is compromised into nothingness before enactment and forgotten thereafter. But an act that clearly poses an issue, and, after open debate, becomes law in a manner that reflects a firm decision of the representatives of the people, possesses a moral authority that is far from negligible. If the responsible officers of government act as if they really believe in its validity, they will communicate that conviction to the rest of the population; and potential offenders will learn to obey, not out of fright, but out of the respect decent Americans bear the accepted standards of the community. That has been the experience of the states with fair employment or education laws; it can be the experience of the nation.

The participants in the civil rights movement who have lost faith in the effectiveness of law and prefer direct action mistakenly interpret the gains of the past decade as signs of fear on the part of the whites. Sit-ins, street demonstrations and the subtle threat of violence are expected to extort concessions that the more orderly processes of politics do not. Where there is no access to the instruments of government, there may be no alternative; but where there is, the preference for the short cut of direct action may have tragic consequences.

The emotion which stirred white Americans who looked at the pictures of marchers knocked over with fire hoses or driven with cattle prods was not fear but fellow feeling. The millions who sympathized were not worried lest the demonstrations spread throughout the country; they responded out of sensitivity to the moral strength of those who suffered and out of concern about the abuse of the law by its custodians. Those feelings might well change if the impression got about that the civil rights movement was willing to use disorder and illegality lightly and under any circumstances.

Fear is the emotion the advocates of equality should least wish to spread; for frightened men will be less likely to respond to ethical considerations than to prepare for self-defense by counterterror. Arbitrary demonstrations, boycotts, pickets and sit-ins will provoke counterdemonstrations, counterboycotts and counterpickets. The support given the initiative petition to repeal California's fair housing law in January 1964 is an ominous indication of the effects of white resentment.

Negroes are one tenth of the nation; nothing could more

effectively unite the other nine tenths against them than the suspicion that the campaign for civil rights will be conducted by other than peaceful means and through other than legal channels, when those are available. The paramount interest of any minority is to establish respect for order; and the Negro who has so often been the victim of violence has a greater stake in excluding it from among the factors that influence policy than anyone else. Otherwise he will supply his enemies with the means of his own destruction. Whatever grievances he may labor under, his best hope of redress is still through a government of law.

It Won't Be Easy — Either Way. The hesitations of the past decade have polarized opinion. The whites of the Deep South are committed to opposing integration. Having glimpsed the possibility of resistance and evasion, they are unwilling to submit to defeat. The Negroes are as fully committed to equality. Having tasted it, they seek their full measure. There are bound to be harsh feelings and distressing incidents and no policy will work which has as its main purpose the mere avoidance of trouble. Someone will have to yield. With regard to the central objective, the time for moderation has passed. More than ever, therefore, it is essential to be prudent in the choice of means, to take care lest the struggle consume the prize and leave only the wreckage of democracy for the victors.

There is not much time. The question we have evaded for a century is now catching up with us. Can a nation which has, in the past, found strength in diversity and freedom in the ability of voluntary groups to coexist in equality now learn to make room for people whose color is the badge of ancient prejudices and injustices? The position of the Negro will not remain fixed; it will either improve as he grasps the opportunities of American society or deteriorate as he fails to do so. Whether conditions permit him to follow one course or the other may prove the crucial test of American democracy.

This is our fire-bell that rings in the night! We must beware of rashness, but with energy and sleepless vigilance go forward to the task — which is no less than the fulfillment of the promise of this Republic, a nation of men made free by equality under the law. To extinguish the fire and rebuild the house on its ancestral foundation is a task worthy of, demanding of, our best efforts.